MATHEMATICS – GETTING IN TOUCH
ACTIVITIES WITH MANIPULATIVES

Book 2

Fredda Friederwitzer

Barbara Berman

Cuisenaire Company of America, Inc.
10 Bank Street. P.O. Box 5026
White Plains, NY 10602-5026

CONTENTS

INTRODUCTION

Why Use Manipulative Materials?   The work of Jean Piaget and others has focused attention on identifying mathematical concepts children can learn and suggesting suitable methods for teaching these ideas. Research indicates that the lack of success many students experience in mathematics may be due to the mode of teaching, not the mathematics being taught! Failure may stem from teaching children with words or symbols initially, instead of with the concrete models they need.

The 125 activities in this book were created as "hands-on" lessons that use materials. The activities are intended to introduce, reinforce, extend or remediate the concepts presented in a basal mathematics program.

How Are Manipulatives Used?   A wide variety of independent strands run through the fabric of elementary and junior high mathematics (i.e. geometry, number, measurement, etc.). Since mathematics is sequential, and new ideas are based upon previously-acquired knowledge, concepts within each strand must be clearly understood in order for students to be successful. This understanding is best developed when children are actively involved in the learning process using all of their senses. The planned use of manipulative materials enables children to "see" basic mathematical relationships, and to understand concepts well enough to use them in solving related problems.

Manipulative materials will not by themselves ensure understanding. Attention must be given to the selection of models suitable to the concept being developed. This book provides activities that use appropriate models to concretely develop mathematical concepts for students.

The Content   In keeping with the authors' philosophy of learning and teaching mathematics, the activities in this book have been developed sequentially. The 125 student activities use manipulative materials and the 30 black line masters in the back of this book. The major topics are covered: Whole Numbers, Addition and Subtraction of Whole Numbers and Money, Multiplication and Division of Whole Numbers, Introduction to Algebra, Fractions and Mixed Numbers, Ratio and Proportion, Decimals and Percent, Geometry, Measurement, and Probability.

How To Use This Book   When using this book, it is important to allow children time to explore the mathematical problems on their own, as well as through teacher questioning for guided discussion.

Although each activity was designed as a self-contained lesson, teachers may discover that the needs of their students require it to occupy several math periods. In contrast, teachers may choose to follow only part of an activity and then return to complete the balance at another time. This flexibility of use extends to the grade level designations as well. An activity designated for fifth grade, for example, may be used by a fourth grade teacher whose class is functioning at an advanced grade level, by a fifth grade teacher to introduce a topic, or by a sixth grade teacher for review and/or remedial work. The needs and abilities of students should determine when and for what purpose an activity is used (introduction, reinforcement, enrichment, or remediation).

Once the teacher has selected the activity or series of activities to follow, the MATERIALS listed should be collected and the needed MASTERS duplicated. It will be helpful to prepare these materials in advance of the lessons and to organize them in envelopes or math-lab boxes.

Grouping for the Activities   All of the activities are designed for use with the whole class, unless small groups or pairs are specified. The teacher can, of course, decide to vary this suggested grouping as student need dictates.

DESCRIPTION OF MATERIALS

POWERS OF TEN: The Powers of Ten materials physically model the place value relationships in our decimal system of numeration. Children can easily verify that one hundred is the same as 10 tens or 100 ones by covering a flat (100) with 10 longs (tens) or 100 units (ones). The Powers of Ten materials allow students to "build" multi-digit numbers, and to model the algorithms for the basic operations. Additional thousands (cubes) can be constructed from Master 7.

COLOR TILES: The Color Tiles are a multi-sensory, multi-purpose material. Concepts of place value, fractions, ratio and proportion, algebra and probability are introduced with the tiles. Basic arithmetic operations are reinforced and extended through use of this material.

FRACTION CIRCLES: The Fraction Circles are a geometric model which help students understand the parts-whole relationship. Each circle, representing one whole cut into halves, thirds, fourths, sixths or eighths, can be taken apart and put back together again. The color, shape, and size of the fractional pieces are visual clues which allow the student to develop a basic understanding of fractional relationships. Concepts of equivalence, mixed numbers and comparing fractions, as well as all operations on fractions, are developed with the Circles. Additional circles can be constructed from Masters 10 and 12.

GEOBOARDS: Students develop a variety of geometric understandings by constructing figures on the geoboard with colored rubberbands. One side, 5 x 5 array of pegs, is used to introduce concepts of perimeter, area, lines, shapes and angles. The circular geoboard on the reverse side allows students to use a concrete model to develop concepts of diameter, radius and circumference.

PRODUCT FINDER BOARDS AND COLOR STRIPS: As students use the Product Finder Boards and Color Strips, they develop familiarity with the multiplication chart and an understanding of place value in multi-digit multiplication examples. A specific color (formed by crossing the Strips on the Board) is assigned to each place (from ones x ones to hundreds x hundreds). Students learn to find partial products of multi-digit examples by color, and combine them to find the complete product.

MONEY: The coins and currency allow children to develop an understanding of our monetary units through concrete experiences. Since the money system we use is decimal-based, these materials are also used to provide alternative models for place value concepts.

MEASUREMENT MATERIALS: Rulers calibrated in centimeters and tape measures (centimeters only) allow children to participate in a variety of linear measurement activities using the metric and customary systems.

WHOLE NUMBERS

Activities 1-6

Activity 1: Reading and Writing Numerals to 2,999

MATERIALS: Powers of Ten Blocks, Cuisenaire Place Value Chart.

Display a variety of numbers through 2,999 on the Cuisenaire Place Value Chart with Powers of Ten materials. Use the Chart to display numbers through 999. Place the thousand cubes to the left of the hundreds' column, off the Chart, to show numbers through 2,999. Have children take turns reading them aloud and writing the numeral and the number word-names on the chalkboard. Use numbers which have zeroes in one or more places. Discuss the relationship between the written zero and the empty place on the chart.

EXTENSION: Display a 3-digit number with Powers of Ten materials not in proper place value sequence. Have children take turns reading the numbers and writing the numeral on the chalkboard.

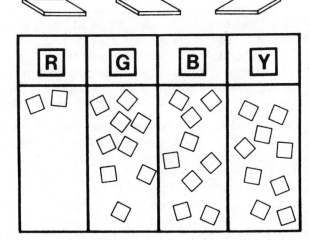

Activity 2: Reading and Writing Numerals to 9,999

MATERIALS: Tiles, Masters 1 and 2.

Relate the tiles to the Powers of Ten materials (i.e. yellow = units, blue = tens, green = hundreds, red = thousands). Repeat Activity 1 using tiles for numbers up to 9,999.

EXTENSIONS: Say a number. Have children display it on Master 2 with tiles, and record the numeral on Master 1.

Write a number in words on the chalkboard. Have children display the number on Master 2 with tiles, and then record the numeral on Master 1.

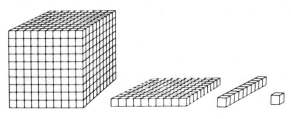

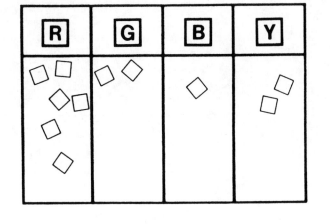

THOUSANDS	HUNDREDS	TENS	ONES

Activity 3: Place Value

MATERIALS: Powers of Ten Blocks, Tiles, Cuisenaire Place Value Chart, Masters 1 and 2.

Write a 3-digit number on the chalkboard. Underline one digit. Working in pairs or groups of three, have children read the number aloud, give the place and value of the underlined digit, and use Power of Ten materials to display it in the appropriate column of the Cuisenaire Place Value Chart. Repeat several times. Extend the activity to 4-digit numbers through 9,999, having children use tiles on Master 2. Numerals which include zero should be used.

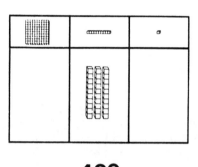

4<u>3</u>9

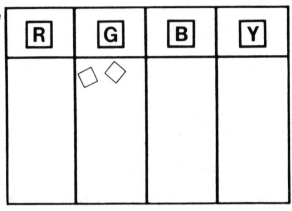

4<u>2</u>18

Activity 4: Build the Greatest Number

MATERIALS: Tiles, Masters 1 and 2.

Play "Build the Greatest Number" using tiles on Master 2. Write a digit from 1-9 on the chalkboard. Children must select color tiles and place them in one of the four columns on Master 2. (See Activity 2 for tile place value designations). Once placed, the tiles cannot be moved. Repeat three more times using different digits. Children record the numeral they have created on Master 1. The greatest number wins. Using the same rules and procedures, play "Build the Smallest Number".

EXTENSION: Have children experiment with tiles on Master 2 to build: the greatest 3-digit number; the greatest 4-digit number; the smallest 3 (or 4) digit number; the greatest number possible using any 2 tiles, 3 tiles, etc.; the smallest number possible using any 6 tiles, 10 tiles etc.; the greatest possible number using only tiles of one color; of two colors. As different solutions are found and presented to the class, children should explain how the solution they are demonstrating meets the criteria set in the problem.

Activity 5: Comparing Numbers to 999

MATERIALS: Powers of Ten Blocks, Money, Master 3, Cuisenaire Place Value Chart.

On the chalkboard, write 16 and 21. Using Powers of Ten materials, have children display each number on a separate number line on Master 3. Ask which is greater, which is less. Repeat for several pairs of 2-digit numbers to 25. Discuss what happens to the numbers as we move to the right on the number line; to the left. On the chalkboard, write a pair of 2-digit numbers (36 and 41). Have children display them with the Power of Ten materials on the Cuisenaire Place Value Chart to decide which is greater. Emphasize that comparing the largest place, in this case tens, helps to decide which number is greater.

   Review the symbols > and <, emphasizing that the open part (or "mouth") always faces the greater number. Children may want to draw a character around the symbol, such as Pac Man, to aid in remembering. Repeat with several number pairs in which the greater number is formed with fewer pieces than the smaller number (36 required 3 tens and 6 units or 9 pieces while 41 needed only 5 pieces). Alternately ask which is greater, which is less, and record on the chalkboard using the appropriate symbol. Continue the activity using number pairs having the same face value but different place values (52 and 25). Repeat the activity for 3-digit numbers (to 999) using Powers of Ten materials or money (bills).

```
0  1  2  3  4  5  6  7  8  9  10  11  12  13  14  15  16  17  18  19  20  21  22  23  24  25
```

```
0  1  2  3  4  5  6  7  8  9  10  11  12  13  14  15  16  17  18  19  20  21  22  23  24  25
```

Activity 6: Comparing Numbers to 9,999

4 5 6 7 8

MATERIALS: Tiles, Powers of Ten Blocks, Cuisenaire Place Value Chart, Money, Master 2.

Repeat Activity 5 for 4-digit numbers using tiles on Master 2. Remember: yellow = units, blue = tens, green = hundreds, and red = thousands. Record on the chalkboard using > and < symbols. Pay special attention to numbers like 2140, 2401; 2014 and 2041. Reinforce the idea of comparing the largest place first, then the next largest, etc. by having children demonstrate their answers with the materials.

EXTENSION: 1) Use tiles on Master 2 to play "Build the Greatest Number" or "Build the Smallest Number" (see Activity 4). As each round is finished, have children record all the numbers they have built on the chalkboard, then order them from greatest to least (or from least to greatest).

2) Say a 2-digit number. Have children display it on the Cuisenaire Place Value Chart with Powers of Ten materials or on Master 2 with money, then record it on the chalkboard. Repeat with two more numbers. Have children compare the numbers and order them from greatest to least; record the order on the chalkboard.

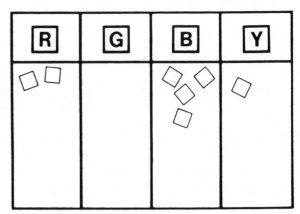

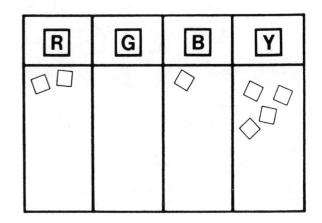

2041 > 2014

ADDING AND SUBTRACTING WHOLE NUMBERS AND MONEY

Activities 7-16

Activity 7: Order (Commutative) Property of Addtion

4 5 6 7 8

MATERIALS: Tiles, Master 4, Crayons.

Have children use tiles of two colors (green and red) to model 3 + 4 on Master 4, and then tell how many tiles in all (7). Similarly, have them model 4 + 3 using the same colors, and tell how many tiles in all (7). Color in the appropriate number of boxes on Master 4 with matching-colored crayons, and write the corresponding fact next to each drawing. Repeat for several other pairs of facts. Point out that the sum is not affected by the order in which the addends are combined. Continue with similar examples, and discuss how this knowledge can be used to check work in addition. CHALLENGE: Ask children to find out if order counts in subtraction by using materials to prove their statements.

EXTENSION: On the chalkboard write a sum. Have children use tiles to show a pair of facts for that sum which model the order (commutative) property of addition.

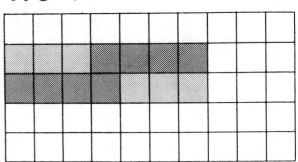

$$3+4=7$$
$$4+3=7$$

Activity 8: Grouping (Associative) Property of Addition

4 5 6 7 8

MATERIALS: Tiles.

Have children use two colors of tiles to display 3 + 4 and find how many in all (7). Add 1 more tile of a different color and find the sum (8). Explain that parentheses can be used to show how the tiles are grouped. Record the number sentence on the chalkboard using parentheses: (3 + 4) + 1. Suggest adding 4 and 1 first, and then 3. Ask how many in all (8), how to use the parentheses to show the grouping 3 + (4 + 1); and whether the sum is still 8. Have children prove their answers using tiles, and write the correct number sentence: 3 + (1 + 4). After several combinations have been tried, tell them to place the three sets of color tiles together. Demonstrate how to regroup the addends in the written number sentence by moving only the parentheses. Repeat with other examples, discussing the grouping of addends. Reiterate that the order in which addends are combined does not affect the sum.

EXTENSION: Have children use tiles of three colors to add 3, 4, and 7 in as many ways as possible, recording each.

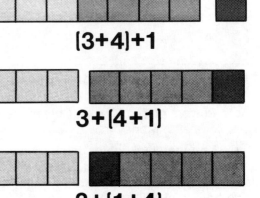

(3+4)+1

3+(4+1)

3+(1+4)

Activity 9: The Zero Property for Addition

4 5 6 7 8

MATERIALS: Tiles.

Have children use tiles of two colors to display addition facts (3 + 2, 1 + 6, etc.). Have children display addition facts with zero by adding zero tiles (3 + 0, 0 + 5, etc). List the addition sentences on the chalkboard. Have children look for a pattern and state a generalization for adding with 0: when zero is one of the addends, the sum is the other addend.

EXTENSION: Repeat the activity for subtraction: 8 − 0, 6 − 0, etc.

Activity 10: Renaming Numbers

4 5 6 7 8

MATERIALS: Powers of Ten Blocks, Cuisenaire Place Value Chart, Tiles, Money, Master 2.

Using Powers of Ten materials and the Cuisenaire Place Value Chart, have children display 245. Ask them to "get" more units without changing the value of the number (trade 1 ten for 10 units), read the value of each place (2 hundreds 3 tens and fifteen ones), and write the expanded numerals on the chalkboard (200 + 30 + 15). Have children reverse the process to again show 245 (200 + 40 + 5). Repeat with tens (1 hundred, 14 tens, 5 units, and then with units and tens (1 hundred, 13 tens, 15 units, etc). On the chalkboard, record all the expanded numerals for 245 that children have displayed. Repeat for other 3 digit numbers paying special attention to numbers like 500, 402, and 670. Stress throughout this activity that although the materials and/or numerals look different, they all represent the same number.

EXTENSION: 1) Repeat the activity with tiles and/or money (dollars, dimes, pennies) on Master 2. Be sure to discuss the trading procedure again using these materials. 2) Repeat the activity for numbers to 2,999 with Powers of Ten material, and for larger numbers using tiles and/or money.

$$200 \; + \; 30 \; + \; 15$$

Activity 11: Addition With and Without Regrouping

4 5 6 7 8

MATERIALS: Powers of Ten Blocks, Cuisenaire Place Value Chart, Tiles, Master 2, Money.

Write 24 + 37 on the chalkboard. Using Powers of Ten materials on the Place Value Chart, have children represent each number. Discuss what the sign (+) tells them to do (add or join), and how they will go about doing it with the materials (join like things, units with units, etc.). Have children join the units and discuss the overloading of the units column. Have them trade 10 units for 1 ten, "carry" the ten to the appropriate column, and then combine tens. Repeat the above procedure for 53 + 29 but this time, record the children's actions on the chalkboard paralleling the addition algorithm. Repeat for other examples: 2 digit + 2 digit numbers; 3 digit + 2 digit numbers; 3 digit + 3 digit numbers; 4 digit + 3 digit numbers. Be sure to include examples that do not require renaming, and those that have renaming in only 1 column.

EXTENSION: Use Master 2 to repeat the activity with tiles and/or money.

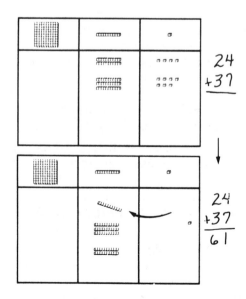

MATERIALS: Two cubes, Powers of Ten Blocks, Tiles, Money, Cuisenaire Place Value Chart, Master 2.

Mark two cubes as follows: Cube one: Blank, 1 dot, 2 dots, 3 dots, 4 dots, 4 dots. Cube two: Blank, I, I, II, III, IIII. The object of the game is to "give away the materials" through exchanging and discarding the number of units or longs indicated by rolling the cubes (dots stand for units, and I for longs). The Cuisenaire Place Value Chart is used as a gameboard. Each player starts with I flat (hundreds) 5 longs (tens), and 5 units (ones). Players roll the two cubes and discard the amounts indicated, exchanging as needed. The game continues as children take turns rolling the cubes and removing the indicated number of pieces from their gameboards. The first player to "clear" the board is the winner. Children should play this game through several times with no notation or recording to acquire A MENTAL IMAGE of the placement of materials and of exchanging. This will give subsequent meaning to subtraction with exchanging.

EXTENSION: Play the game with tiles and/or money on Master 2. Be sure to mark the columns on Master 2, and the cubes, to match accordingly.

Play the game starting from 1,000 to 2,000 (red tiles); $1,000 or $2,000, etc. When beginning with a large number, the goal should be changed (e.g., starting with 3,000 the winner must reach 1,800) and/or the cubes should be remarked to include 100's.

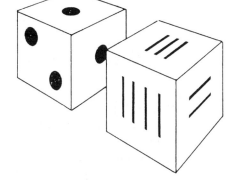

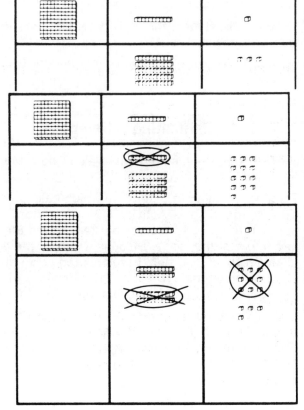

MATERIALS: Powers of Ten Blocks, Tiles, Money, Cuisenaire Place Value Chart, Master 2.

Write 53 − 29 in vertical form on the chalkboard. Ask children what needs to be displayed with materials to solve the example (53). Discuss taking 9 away, why it can't be done, and what should be done (trade a ten for 10 units.) Count how many tens there are (4), and how many units (13). Ask if the value of 4 tens and 13 units is equal to the value of 5 tens and 3 units. Complete the example taking away 9 units and 2 longs. Have children tell what's left. Repeat several times with no writing. Include some examples where renaming is NOT necessary. Record the children's actions with materials by writing each step on the chalkboard.

Repeat with other examples including 50 − 29, 54 − 7; with 3 through 6-digit numbers in the minuend, and with 1-6-digits in the subtrahend. Also include problems with zeroes in various places.

EXTENSION: Use tiles and/or money on Master 2. This activity is especially good for making change from $1 to $20 bills.

Activity 14: Rounding Numbers

MATERIALS: Money, Master 2.

Write 73¢ on the chalkboard. Discuss the concept of rounding (i.e., approximating) with respect to the price of an item. Have children display 73¢ with dimes and pennies on Master 2. Ask if 73¢ is closer to 70¢ or 80¢. Have them prove it using the materials. Make a chart of other amounts (except 75¢) on the chalkboard. Have children study the chart to find the pattern (i.e. 70¢-74¢ are closer to 70¢, and 76¢-79¢ are closer to 80¢). Count how many amounts are closer to 70¢ (5); to 80¢ (4). What amount is missing from the chart (75¢)? To which amount is it closer (neither; midway). To keep things even, to which group should it be assigned (80¢)? Add 75¢ to the chart. Discuss the accepted convention for rounding. Repeat the activity with amounts like $1.70, $1.84, and then with numbers like 170 and 184.

EXTENTION: Repeat the activity for 4 and 5 digit numbers and amounts to $10,000.

Rounding Chart	
ACTUAL AMOUNT:	CLOSER TO:
73¢	70¢
78¢	80¢
71¢	70¢
74¢	70¢
79¢	80¢
76¢	80¢
70¢	70¢
77¢	80¢
75¢	?

Activity 15: Estimating Sums

MATERIALS: Money, Master 2.

Write "38¢ + 43¢" on the chalkboard. Discuss the need to approximate the sum to determine if $1 will cover the purchases. Review rounding (see Activity 14). On Master 2, have children display each amount, rounding to the nearest dime, and then add, recording the sum. Have children then display the original amounts and add. Compare the two sums. Discuss how close they are. Repeat several times for other money amounts. Repeat for sums using numbers up to 100.

EXTENSION: Repeat the activity for amounts from $1 to $1,000, and for numbers over 100.

Repeat the activity for three or four addends (using money or numbers).

Activity 16: Estimating Differences

MATERIALS: Cuisenaire Place Value Chart, Money.

Write "46 − 28 = 28" and "46 − 28 = 18" on the chalkboard. Discuss the need to determine which calculation is accurate. (Review rounding – Activity 14.) Have children represent each number, rounded to the nearest ten, on the Place Value Chart and find the difference. Discuss which of the original answers is closer to 18, and then have children solve the original problem with materials. Discuss the closeness of the answer to the estimate. Repeat for several other similar examples.

EXTENSION: Solve problems which involve making change from a $1-$20 bill. Have children round the purchase amount and then act out the problem with a friend, using paper currency.

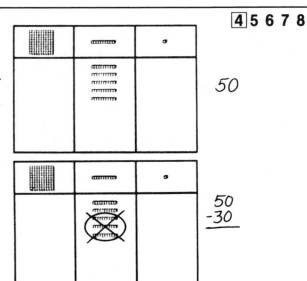

INTRODUCTION TO ALGEBRA
(ADDITION AND SUBTRACTION)

Activities 17-18

Activity 17: Introduction to Algebra: Addition Number Sentences

MATERIALS: Tiles and Envelopes.

Secretly place 6 tiles in an envelope. Show the envelope and display 5 more tiles to the right of it. Explain that there are 11 tiles altogether. Record this by writing "envelope $+5 = 11$". Ask how many tiles are in the envelope (6), and what operation was used to solve the question (subtraction).

Write the number sentence using "n" for the unknown number of tiles: $n + 5 = 11$. Repeat the activity with different numbers.

GAME: Distribute one envelope and 15 tiles to each pair of children. Player 1 sets up a number sentence as above using tiles and the envelope, and then writes the appropriate equation. Player 2 writes the related subtraction number sentence and then solves for n. In the next round, roles are reversed.

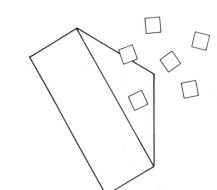

Activity 18: Introduction to Algebra: Subtraction Number Sentences

MATERIALS: Tiles and Envelopes.

Secretly place 15 tiles in an envelope. Show the children that 8 tiles are being removed from the envelope while 7 tiles remain inside. To record, write "envelope $- 8 = 7$". Ask how many tiles were in the envelope originally (15). Discuss how the number sentence was solved (addition). Place the 7 tiles and the 8 tiles together to show 15 tiles. Have children write a number sentence for the original problem using "n" for the unknown number of tiles instead of "envelope": $n - 8 = 7$, then write the related number sentence used to solve: $n = 7 + 8$. Repeat the activity using different numbers.

GAME: Distribute 1 envelope and 15 tiles to each pair of children. Player 1 sets up a number sentence as above using as many tiles as s/he wishes in the envelope, and then removes some tiles. Player 2 writes the appropriate number sentence, and then uses the tiles to solve for n. In the next round, roles are reversed.

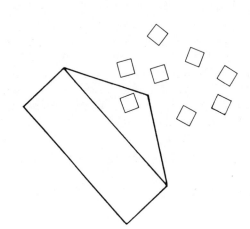

MULTIPLICATION OF WHOLE NUMBERS

Activities 19-36

Activity 19: Basic Multiplication Facts Using Sets

4 5 6 7 8

MATERIALS: Tiles.

Have children work in pairs. Stack (or group) tiles to show 1 set of 3, 2 sets of 3, through 10 sets of 3. Ask them to find the total number of tiles in each set by pointing to and counting the stacks aloud by 3's. Record the information on the chalkboard, and use it to review the terms "factor" and "product" (i.e. "Circle the product of 4 x 3". "Put a triangle around the factors of 12", etc.). Repeat the activity to develop (or review) multiplication facts through 10 x 10.

Activity 20: Basic Multiplication Facts Using Arrays

4 5 6 7 8

MATERIALS: Tiles, Master 4, Product Finder Board and Color Strips.

Have children set out 1 row of 3 tiles and beneath it another row of 3 tiles. Ask how many rows, how many tiles in each row, and how many in all. Record on the chalkboard using words and numerals. Give a fact, e.g., 3 x 4. Reiterate that the first factor in a multiplication sentence indicates the number of rows, and the second factor tells how many in each row. Have children set up the array using tiles (e.g. 3 rows of 4 tiles). Repeat for facts through 10 x 10.

EXTENSION: Repeat the activity, having children display multiplication facts by placing tiles on Master 4, and outlining the array. As a fact is completed, children should lift the tile in the lower right-hand corner and record the product number in that space. Master 4 should be labeled and used as a multiplication chart (for facts through 10 x 7).

Use the product finder board and the yellow colored strips to review and reinforce the basic multiplication facts.

4X3 = 12   3X4 = 12

X	1	2	3	4	5	6	7	8	9	10
1	1	2	3	4	5	6	7	8	9	10
2	2	4	6	8	10	12	14	16	18	20
3	3	6	9	12	15	18	21	24	27	30
4	4	8	12	16	20	24	28	32	36	40
5	5	10	15	20	25	30	35	40	45	50
6	6	12	18	24	30	36	42	48	54	60
7	7	14	21	28	35	42	49	56	63	70
8	8	16	24	32	40	48	56	64	72	80
9	9	18	27	36	45	54	63	72	81	90
10	10	20	30	40	50	60	70	80	90	100

Activity 21: Zero Property of Multiplication

4 5 6 7 8

MATERIALS: Master 5, Unit Cubes.

Ask children to use unit cubes to display two sets of 2 and then 1 set of 2. Record 2 x 2 = 4 and 1 x 2 = 2 on the chalkboard. Then ask them to display 0 sets of 2 and record as 0 x 2 =   . Discuss why 0 sets of 2 cannot be displayed, emphasizing the meaning of 0 sets as "no sets". Continue similarly to develop the facts for multiplication by 0 (from 0 x 1 through 0 x 10), recording in a column on the chalkboard. Have children study the column, look for a pattern and then generalize that 0 times any number is 0.

2X2   1X2   0X2

Ask children to display 3 sets of 2, of 1, of 0. Record 3 x 2 = 6, 3 x 1 = 3, 3 x 0 = 0 on the chalkboard. Discuss why 3 x 0 cannot be displayed, emphasizing that the 0 set means that there are "no cubes" in each set. Record the solution (0) for the example. Develop the multiplication facts (from 1 x 0 through 10 x 0), recording them in a column on the chalkboard to the right of the (0 x ...) facts. Have children study the columns of examples, and look for a pattern, and generalize that 0 times any number is 0.

3X2   **3X1**   **3X0**

Activity 22: Identity Property of Multiplication

4 5 6 7 8

MATERIALS: Unit Cubes, Master 5.

Have children use unit cubes to display 1 set of 4. Ask how many sets, and how many cubes in the set. Record on the chalkboard. Have children display 1 set of 1, 1 set of 3, etc., through 1 set of 10, recording each example and answer in a column. Have children study the column, look for patterns, and make a generalization, i.e., one times any number is that number.

1×1
1×2
1×3
1×4
1×5

Have children display 2 sets of 1. Record on the chalkboard as 2 x 1 = 2. Ask how many sets, and how many are in the set. Record the answer (2): 2 x 1 = 2. Continue similarly with 3 x 1 etc., recording the examples in a column. Have children inspect the recorded facts for a pattern, and generalize that any number times 1 is equal to that number.

☐1×1 ☐2×1 ☐3×1 ☐4×1 ☐5×1

Activity 23: Order (Commutative) Property of Multiplication

4 5 6 7 8

MATERIALS: Unit Cubes, Masters 4, 5 and 6, Scissors, Tiles.

Have children display a 3 x 4 array on Master 4 with the tiles. Ask how many rows, how many in each row, and how many tiles in all? Have them trace around the array, remove the tiles, and mark "3 x 4 = 12" inside the rectangle. Repeat for an array of 4 x 3. After marking the resulting rectangle "4 x 3 = 12", have children cut out both rectangles and compare them for similarities and differences.

Repeat with other examples through 10 x 7. List the pairs of multiplication facts which have the same product. Have children study the list, look for a pattern, and generalize that the order of the factors does not affect the product (i.e. multiplication is commutative).

Call out a multiplication fact (e.g., 4 x 7). Have children display it using cubes on Master 6, outlining the rectangle and writing the number sentence inside. Ask them to display the "related" array WITHOUT rearranging the cube, (i.e. by turning Master 6 one quarter turn) then give the appropriate number sentence.

Challenge children to discover multiplication sentences that have only 1 array (i.e. 1 x 1, 2 x 2, etc.). Have them display and explain their discoveries using units on Master 6 . Discuss the shape of these arrays (square) and how they differ from those created earlier (rectangles).

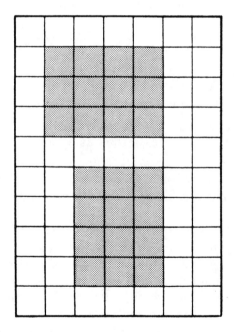

EXTENSION: On the chalkboard, write a product (i.e. 15). Have children take that number of unit cubes, and build a rectangular array on Master 6, trace around the array, remove the cubes, and record the multiplication sentence inside. Below, outline the rectangle that would be formed using the commutative multiplication fact and write the fact inside. Check using the cubes. Have children find as many multiplication pairs for a given product as they can.

On the multiplication chart (Master 5) have children box off the square numbers. Discuss the line formed through the chart by these numbers (i.e. a diagonal). Have children fold the chart on the diagonal and hold it up to the light. Notice that like products match in position. Discuss why (because of the commutative property of multiplication, the products of 6 x 8 and 8 x 6 match).

Activity 24: Grouping (Associative) Property of Multiplication 4 [5] 6 7 8

MATERIALS: Unit Cubes.

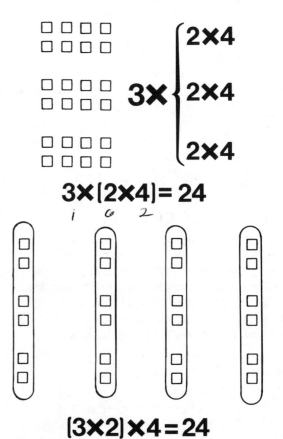

Have children display a 2 x 4 array with unit cubes. Ask how many rows (2), and how many cubes in each row (4). Record on chalkboard as: 2 x 4. Have children repeat the display twice more, recording each display on the chalkboard. Ask how many arrays are displayed (3), what are the factors in each array (2 and 4), and record on the chalkboard as 3 x (2 x 4). Point out that the parentheses are used to identify the content of each array. Ask how many cubes in one array (8), how many cubes in all (24) and record the simplified expression below the first one: 3 x 8 = 24.

Have children leave the arrays intact and continue the activity by writing (3 x 2) x 4 on the chalkboard. Ask children to simplify this expression by "clearing" parentheses. Record the simplified expression, 6 x 4 below the original and review the meaning of each of its factors (see Activity 20). Have children use cubes to display 6 x 4 as an array. Ask how many cubes were used in all (24), how many in one row (4), and how many rows (6). Have children compare this display with the previous one, noting that both contain 24 cubes and set up in 6 rows of 4. The two displays differ in the way the rows of 4 are grouped. Compare the two original written expressions, pointing out that the grouping of factors by parentheses does not change the final product, although the physical appearance of each display is slightly different. Repeat for other expressions, e.g. 2 x (4 x 1) and (2 x 4) x 1.

Activity 25: Distributive Property of Multiplication [4] 5 6 7 8

MATERIALS: Tiles.

Have children display 2 + 4 using 2 red and 4 green tiles. Ask how many tiles in all (6). Have them repeat the display twice more, asking how many sets of 2 + 4 are displayed in all. Record on the chalkboard as 3 x (2 + 4) = . Discuss how many red tiles (6), how many green tiles (12), and how many tiles in all (18). What multiplication fact do the red tiles show (3 x 2)? What multiplication fact do the green tiles show (3 x 4)? Record on the chalkboard as (3 x 2) + (3 x 4) = . Compare the

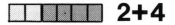 2+4

two number sentences, indicating that they are the same. Explain that 3 x (2 + 4) can be seen as 3 groups of 6 tiles each, while (3 x 2) + (3 x 4) is 3 groups of 2 (red) and 3 groups of 4 (green). Have children find the product of each number sentence (18), and discuss the meaning of the distributive property of multiplication over addition.

Repeat the activity, having children use tiles to display 4 x (3 + 1), and then model the distributive property by displaying (4 x 3) + (4 x 1). Discuss the operation of the distributive property again for this example and repeat with several others.

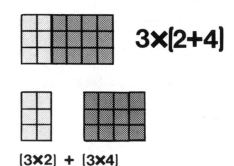

3×(2+4)

(3×2) + (3×4)

Activity 26: Multiplying With Tens

4 5 6 7 8

MATERIALS: Powers of Ten Blocks, Cuisenaire Place Value Chart, Master 2, Money (dimes and dollar bills).

Display 2 tens in the appropriate column of the Cuisenaire Place Value Chart. Ask how many tens (2), how many ones (0), and record this information on the chalkboard in tabular form. Repeat for 4 tens, 7 tens, etc. (through 9 tens), recording similarly. Have children study the table to find a pattern and discuss their observations. Emphasize the 0 in the ones column during the discussion, relating it to the absence of any units. Continue the activity, displaying 10 tens, 11 tens, 15 tens, 18 tens, 20 tens, 23 tens, etc., recording each action on the chalkboard table. Ask if the same pattern appears on the table. Develop a generalization about what happens when ten is multiplied by any number.

Have children display 10 groups of 2 in the units column on the Cuisenaire Place Value Chart, make the necessary trades, and CARRY the tens to the appropriate column. Verbalize the actions as they are performed. Record on the chalkboard in tabular form. Repeat for 10 fives, 10 eights, etc. through 10 tens, recording similarly. Have children look for a pattern in the table, and discuss what happens when a number is multiplied by 10. Continue the activity for 10 elevens, 10 thirteens, 10 twenties, etc., recording on the chalkboard table. Refer to the pattern discussed earlier and ask if it still appears. Reiterate the generalization for multiplication by 10.

EXTENSION: Repeat the activity with dimes and dollars on Master 2.

Have children find the piece that is equal to 10 tens (the flat) and tell its value (100). Record on the chalkboard as 10 tens = 100 or 10 x 10 = 100. Have them use hundred flats to build 20 tens, 30 tens, 50 tens, etc., find the total value, and record it on the chalkboard. Generalize the rule for multiplying tens by tens, and have the children use it to find 30 x 20, 20 x 20, 20 x 50, etc.

Multiplying with TENS	
2 Tens	20
3 Tens	30
5 Tens	50
7 Tens	70
15 Tens	150
23 Tens	230

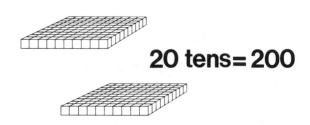

20 tens = 200

Activity 27: Multiplying With Hundreds and Thousands

4 5 6 7 8

MATERIALS: Powers of Ten Blocks, Cuisenaire Place Value Chart, Masters 2 and 7, Scissors, Money (bills).

Repeat Activity 26 using hundred flats on the Cuisenaire Place Value Chart or $100 bills on Master 2 to develop a generalization for multiplying by hundreds. Have children construct a thousand cube from Master 7. Display one thousand cube to the left of the hundreds' column and off the Cuisenaire Place Value Chart. Ask how many thousands, hundreds, tens, and ones are shown on the chart and record the number on a chalkboard table. Repeat with two, three, four cubes, etc. recording each action on the chalkboard. Continue the activity by presenting verbal examples, and have children respond orally. Record their responses on the chalkboard table (8 thousands, 14 thousands, 20 thousands, etc.). Discuss the pattern that emerges, and develop a rule for multiplying by thousands.

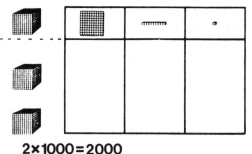

$2 \times 1000 = 2,000$
$14 \times 1000 = 14,000$

Activity 28: Multiplication of Two and Three-Digit Numbers By a One-Digit Number Without Regrouping

MATERIALS: Powers of Ten Blocks, Cuisenaire Place Value Chart, Product Finder Board and Color Strips, Master 8, Crayons (orange and grey or silver).

Have children display 2 groups of 23 on the Cuisenaire Place Value Chart using Powers of Ten materials. Ask how many groups of 23, and record their response on the chalkboard. Have them combine the ones on the chart, and record the partial product on the chalkboard. Then combine the tens, find their value, and record that partial product. Ask how many in all. Continue similarly for various two-digit x one-digit combinations with no regrouping. Repeat the activity with a three-digit number.

EXTENSION: Children should solve similar examples, using Powers of Ten materials on the chart, and then check the solution using the Product Finder Board and Color Strips.

Have children display 3 groups of 23 with Powers of Ten materials on Master 8 (held horizontally). Pictorially record the image by removing one ten at a time and coloring the space it occupied with an orange crayon. Remove the ones, coloring the spaces they occupied with a silver or grey crayon. Record these actions on the chalkboard using the partial product algorithm. Repeat several times, using combinations of one digit x two and three-digit numbers (such as 2 x 123, 3 x 32) with no regrouping.

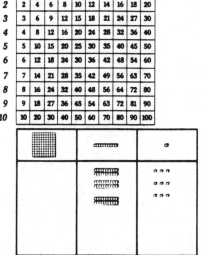

X	1	2	3	4	5	6	7	8	9	10
1	1	2	3	4	5	6	7	8	9	10
2	2	4	6	8	10	12	14	16	18	20
3	3	6	9	12	15	18	21	24	27	30
4	4	8	12	16	20	24	28	32	36	40
5	5	10	15	20	25	30	35	40	45	50
6	6	12	18	24	30	36	42	48	54	60
7	7	14	21	28	35	42	49	56	63	70
8	8	16	24	32	40	48	56	64	72	80
9	9	18	27	36	45	54	63	72	81	90
10	10	20	30	40	50	60	70	80	90	100

Activity 29: Piling It Up

MATERIALS: Powers of Ten Blocks, 5-Sector Spinner Marked 1, 2, 3, 4, 5.

Children play in groups of 2-4 starting with 2 units each. Remaining materials are placed in a "bank" in the center of the group. The spinner is used to indicate how many PILES of two cubes must be made. If the first player spins a 4, s/he makes 4 piles with 2 cubes in each, and combines the piles to find the total (8). Play continues around the group. On the next turn, the first player forms piles of 8 cubes, combines the piles and exchanges from units to tens if necessary to find the new total (perhaps 16). The next turn would require groups of 16 to be formed, combined and, if necessary, exchanged. Play continues until one player has 5 flats. Repeat as frequently as needed, without any recording, to develop the idea of multiplication with regrouping.

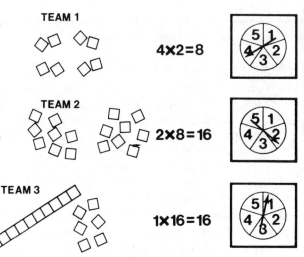

TEAM 1 $4 \times 2 = 8$

TEAM 2 $2 \times 8 = 16$

TEAM 3 $1 \times 16 = 16$

Activity 30: Multiplication With Regrouping I

MATERIALS: Powers of Ten Blocks, Cuisenaire Place Value Chart, Product Finder Board and Color Strips.

Have children display 3 groups of 126 on their Place Value Chart and record on the chalkboard as 3 x 126. Have them combine the ones, move them down to the bottom of the Chart, exchange 10 ones for one ten, and record the partial product on the chalkboard. Repeat for the tens and for the hundreds, and find the total product. Repeat the activity in a similar way for two and three-digit x one-digit number combinations which require regrouping from ones to tens. Use the Product Finder Boards and Color Strips to check the partial products and solutions.

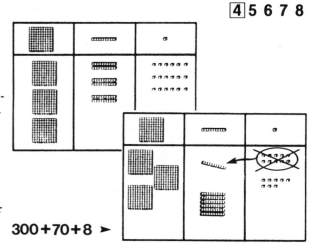

300+70+8 ►

Activity 31: Multiplication With Regrouping II

MATERIALS: Powers of Ten Blocks, Product Finder Board and Color Strips, Master 8, Crayons (orange and grey or silver).

Write 13 x 15 on the chalkboard. Have children explain what it means (i.e. 13 groups of 15), and then display it with Powers of Ten materials on Master 8. Refer to the array of 15 unit cubes and ask what fact it shows. Record the partial product: 15 (3 x 5). Point to the 3 adjacent tens. Identify the multiplication sentence they display, show it in the chalkboard example, and record the partial product: 30 (3 x 10). Ask how many more ones are displayed (50), how many rows (10), and how many in each row (5). Show this in the example, and record the partial product: 50 (10 x 5). Continue to the hundred flat which covers ten tens. Show it in the example and record the partial product 100 (10 x 10). Add the partial products, and check the solution by counting the displayed materials. Try other examples such as 22 x 18, 4 x 123, etc. Use the Product Finder Board and Color Strips to double check solutions and reinforce the partial product algorithm.

EXTENSION: After children display materials on Master 8, remove the pieces and color the spaces to record the action.

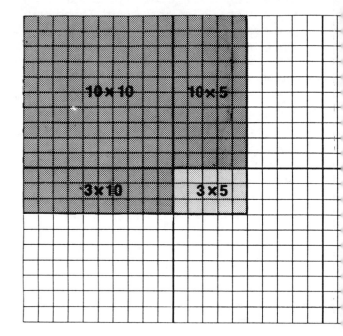

Activity 32: Finding Multiples

MATERIALS: Tiles, Master 9.

Have children use green tiles to show arrays for the multiplication facts of 1 x 3 through 5 x 3. Read the products aloud (3, 6, 9, 12, 15). Repeat with red tiles to show arrays for the multiplication facts of 1 x 2 through 5 x 2. Read the products aloud. Introduce the term "multiple" as a special name for these products. Ask children how many multiples of 2 are displayed (5). What is the next multiple of 2 (12), the next multiple of 3 (18), or the eighth multiple of 2, etc. Using blue tiles, have children display the first three multiples of 4 and read the products aloud (4, 8, 12). Tell what multiple of 4 is next and display it. On Master 9, have them use a green crayon to circle

12

---

the first 5 multiples of 3, referring to the arrays of green tile if needed. Use a red crayon to triangle the first 5 multiples of 2, referring to the red tile arrays if needed. Discuss any numbers which are marked with both a circle and a triangle. Introduce the term "common multiple", and list on the chalkboard the common multiples found for 2 and 3 thus far (6). Have children continue triangling the multiples of 2 in red, through 24. Record the common multiples of 2 and 3 (6, 12, 18, 24).

EXTENSION: On the same Master, have children draw a blue x on the first six multiples of 4 referring to the blue tile arrays if needed. Discuss the multiples common to 2, 3, and 4 (12, 24), and find the lowest multiple common to all (12). Introduce the term "Least or Lowest Common Multiple" or LCM. On a clean copy of Master 6, have children circle the first ten multiples of 5 and x the first ten multiples of 4. Find the common multiples and the LCM. Repeat as needed for other multiplication tables.

91	92	93	94	95	96	97	98	99	100
81	82	83	84	85	86	87	88	89	90
71	72	73	74	75	76	77	78	79	80
61	62	63	64	65	66	67	68	69	70
51	52	53	54	55	56	57	58	59	60
41	42	43	44	45	46	47	48	49	50
31	32	33	34	35	36	37	38	39	40
21	22	23	24	25	26	27	28	29	30
11	12	13	14	15	16	17	18	19	20
1	2	3	4	5	6	7	8	9	10

Activity 33: Introducing Factors, Primes and Composites

MATERIALS: Tiles, Unit Cubes, Master 9.

Have children use 12 tiles to make as many rectangular arrays as they can. Have them tell the appropriate multiplication fact for each array and record on the chalkboard 4 x 3, 3 x 4, 12 x 1, etc. Introduce the term "factor" by relating it to the "facts" recorded. From the list of facts, have children tell the different factors of 12 (1, 2, 3, etc.). Point out that it is not necessary to repeat a factor even if it occurs in several multiplication facts. Make a chalkboard chart showing the facts and factors. Repeat the activity for 6, 3, 10, 16.

Ask children to make all possible rectangular arrays for 2, 5, 8, 7, 15 with tiles. Discuss how many were made for each number. Separate the numbers used into two groups - those that have only two rectangular arrays and those that have more than two. Develop a chalkboard chart showing both groups of numbers. Introduce the terms "prime number" for the former and "composite number" for the latter. Add "Primes" and "Composites" to the chart in the appropriate columns.

Ask children whether 12 is a prime or a composite number and why. Have children identify the numbers factored earlier (i.e. 6, 3, 10, 16) as prime or composite and list on the chart. Have children transfer the information from the chart to Master 9 by circling all the prime numbers discovered. Have them investigate the remaining numbers through 20 to determine which are prime and circle them on Master 9. (See extension for a discussion of 0 and 1.)

EXTENSION: Introduce the use of division as another way to find the factors of a number. Have children take 32 unit cubes and divide them into two equal groups, three equal groups, etc. Record the division sentences for each action. Reiterate that one number is a factor of another, only if it divides the first number evenly, with no remainder. Circle all division sentences with no remainders. Relate the term "factor" to multiplication facts by having children tell the multiplication sentence which matches the circled division sentence.

Have children use tiles to make rectangular arrays from 0 to 1. Discuss the fact that 0 and 1 are special since no arrays can be made for 0 and only one array can be made for 1. These numbers are not considered prime or composite.

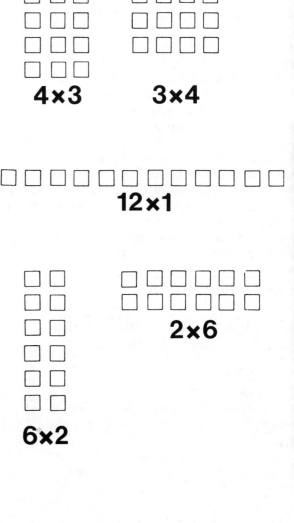

4x3   3x4

12x1

2x6

6x2

Activity 34: Greatest Common Factor

4 5 6 7 8

MATERIALS: Unit Cubes.

Review finding the factors of a number (Activity 33). Have children use unit cubes to find the factors of 8 and 12. Record them on the chalkboard. Circle the factors COMMON to both 8 and 12. Underline the GREATEST of the common factors. Repeat with different number pairs; with three numbers.

Activity 35: Powers (Exponents)

4 5 6 7 8

MATERIALS: Powers of Ten Blocks.

Have children use unit cubes to make 3 x 3, 4 x 4, and 5 x 5 arrays. Discuss the shape, the number of rows, the number of units in each row, and the total number of units in the array. Record the information on a chalkboard chart. Have children look across each row of the chart for the pattern. Introduce the exponential notation, 3^2, as a shorthand for writing 3 x 3 and add it to the chart. Point out that it is read as "3 squared". Ask children to explain why this is so. Have children enter the exponential notation for the other numbers on the chart and read each aloud. Have them "make" other squared numbers through 10^2, recording the expanded and exponential form for each on the chart. Have children cover the 10 x 10 square with longs or a flat. Discuss the equality of each.

SHAPE	NUMBER OF ROWS	NUMBER PER ROW	TOTAL	NOTATION
SQUARE	3	3	9	3^2
SQUARE	4	4	16	4^2
SQUARE	5	5	25	5^2
SQUARE	10	10		

Pile 10 flats up, one on the other to form a "building". Have children figure out how many units (or rooms) the "building" has, and explain how they did so. Discuss ways of recording this action. Since each flat or "floor" is 10 units x 10 units (100 units), and there are 10 floors, the action can be recorded as 10 units x 10 units x 10 units (or 1,000 units). Record this on a chalkboard chart. Introduce the exponential notation 10^3. Ask children to explain why it is read as "10 cubed". Have children display 3^2 with unit cubes. Ask for the number of rooms on this floor (9), and the number of floors needed to show 3^3. Have children build 3^3 and determine how many units it has. Record on the chart. Repeat for 4^3, 2^3, etc.

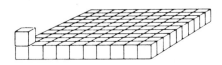

Activity 36: Rounding and Estimating

4 5 6 7 8

MATERIALS: Powers of Ten Blocks, Cuisenaire Place Value Chart, Money.

Review rounding to the nearest ten (dime) or hundred (dollar) as in Activity 14. Write 3 x 64¢ on the chalkboard. Discuss the use of estimation to approximate the amount needed for purchasing 3 items. Have children round 64¢ to the nearest ten (dime), and display 3 x the ROUNDED amount using coins. Perform the necessary trades, and record the estimated product. Then, have them display the same problem with Powers of Ten materials, combine, perform the necessary trades, and record the product. Have them compare the two results. Repeat for other products of two-digit numbers (rounding to the nearest ten or dime), and three-digit numbers (rounding to the nearest hundred or dollar).

DIVISION OF WHOLE NUMBERS

Activities 37-47

Activity 37: Basic Division Facts

4 5 6 7 8

MATERIALS: Paper Cups and Tiles.

Take 3 cups. Count out 18 tiles. Ask how many tiles could be put evenly into each cup. Have children place the tiles, one by one, into each of the 3 cups. Ask for the division sentence that shows this action (18 ÷ 3 = □ or 3⟌18). Ask them to show the related multiplication sentence (3 x □ = 18). Repeat the procedure using 6 cups and 18 tiles, showing the division sentence (18 ÷ 6 = □ or 6⟌18), and the related multiplication sentence (6 x □ = 18). In both cases, we know how many cups (groups) there are. We are trying to find how many tiles in each group, and compare the division sentence to its related multiplication sentence.

Take 18 tiles. Ask how many cups will be needed if 3 tiles are put into each cup. Distribute the tiles and ask for the division sentence that shows the action (18 ÷ 3 = □ or 3⟌18). Ask to show the related multiplication sentence (□ x 3 = 18). Point out that the division sentence looks the same as the first example, and ask why the multiplication sentences are different. (In the first example we are looking for <u>how many in each cup.</u> In the second, we know how many in each cup and we are looking for <u>the number of cups.</u>) Continue this activity with different examples having children write the division sentence and the related multiplication sentence.

18 ÷ 3 = □

Activity 38: Extending Division Concepts

4 5 6 7 8

MATERIALS: Powers of Ten Blocks and Cups.

Display 48 with Powers of Ten materials. Ask how to divide the materials evenly among 4 cups. Children may suggest distributing the pieces starting with the ones or the tens. Accept either way. Ask how much will be in each cup (12). Do the same for the division (48 ÷ 4 = 12 or 4⟌48, and for the related multiplication (4 x □ = 48).

Write 45 ÷ 3 on the chalkboard. Ask what the number sentence means (distribute 45 into 3 groups), and how to show it. Children will probably display 4 tens and 5 ones, and then distribute the pieces into 3 cups starting with the ones. After putting 1 unit into each cup, they should notice the need to trade a ten for 10 ones in order to continue distributing the pieces evenly among the cups.

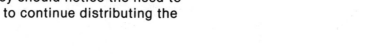

Display the 45 again. Have children distribute the materials into 3 cups starting with the tens. Record the "action" as the number is being divided. Ask which way was more efficient. Emphasize that distributing should start from the largest place. Write several examples on the chalkboard. Have children display the appropriate materials and distribute them into cups.

Activity 39: Division With Remainders

4 5 6 7 8

MATERIALS: Tiles and Cups, Powers of Ten Blocks, Money (dimes and pennies).

Distribute 18 tiles among 4 cups, and have children tell the division sentence (18 ÷ 4 = □ or 4)18). After placing four tiles in each cup, 2 tiles will be left. Ask if the two tiles could be put evenly into each cup (No). Thus, there are 4 tiles in each cup with 2 left over. Introduce the term remainder, and the convention of writing 4R2 as the quotient.

Write 21 ÷ 5 = □ on the chalkboard. Have children solve the example by dividing tiles into the cups. Record the quotient on the chalkboard. Write several more examples alternating the format (i.e. 21 ÷ 5 = □ or 5)21). Include examples that have no remainders. Discuss the concept of divisibility. (If a number can be evenly divided by another with no remainder, then it is said to be divisible by that number.)

EXTENSION: Repeat the activity using Powers of Ten materials.

Repeat the activity using dimes and pennies.

$$18 \div 4 = 4\,R2$$

Activity 40: The Repeated Subtraction Model for Division

4 5 6 7 8

MATERIALS: Powers of Ten Blocks and Cups.

Display 12 with Powers of Ten Materials and write 12 ÷ 4 = □ on the chalkboard. Ask children to divide the materials by placing 4 units in a cup. Children should suggest trading 1 ten for 10 units in order to complete the task. Ask them to find the number of cups needed.

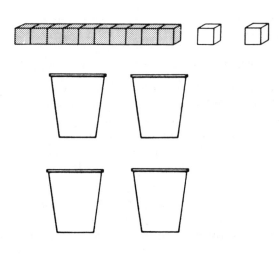

Activity 41: Divide Down (A Game for groups of 2-4 players)

MATERIALS: Powers of Ten Blocks, a Cube or Spinner marked 1, 2, 2, 3, 3, 4.

Directions: Players start with five flats (hundreds) and take turns rolling the die. The number rolled tells how many equal piles the five flats must be divided into. Players divide their pieces into the indicated number of piles evenly, exchanging as necessary. They keep the contents of only one of the divided piles to play the next round. Play continues until one player has 2 (or fewer) units and wins the game.

Example: A player has "Divided Down" until s/he has 166, then rolls a "4". The one flat would be exchanged for ten longs, one long for ten ones, and four piles, as shown, should be made. One pile of "41" is kept for the next round.

Children should play this game initially without notation and then by keeping score. Example: First round, each player starts with 500. The first player rolls "3". After making necessary trades to divide the materials evenly, s/he records 3$\overline{)500}$ = 166R2. On the next round that player starts with 166 and rolls "4", s/he divides the 166 into 4 piles, and records 4$\overline{)166}$ = 41R2. Play would continue until one player had 2 or fewer units.

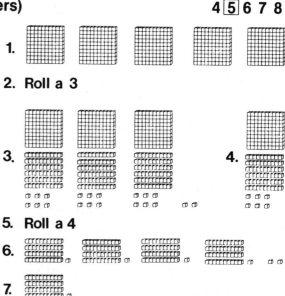

1.

2. Roll a 3

3.   4.

5. Roll a 4

6.

7.

Activity 42: The Division Algorithm

MATERIALS: Powers of Ten Blocks and Cups, Tiles, Money (pennies, dimes, dollars).

Write 7$\overline{)238}$ on the chalkboard. Discuss the possible interpretations of the example: 1) distributing 238 into 7 cups; 2) putting 7 in each cup. Decide which interpretation would be easier to model with the Powers of Ten materials (first), and discuss why. Have children carry out the action with Powers of Ten materials, reminding them to start with the "largest" pieces, (the hundreds). Encourage children to trade the flats (2 hundreds) for 20 tens. Ask how many tens (23), have them distribute the tens, and tell how many tens in each cup (3). Ask how many tens are left (2). Ask how much remains to distribute (28), and what should be done (trade the 2 tens for 20 ones), and distribute the 28 ones. Have them tell how many ones (4), and the total amount in each cup (24).

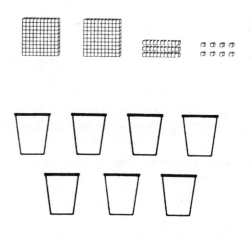

Repeat with another similar example, e.g. 6$\overline{)318}$; this time parellel the "actions" with the conventional algorithm for division. Have children work in pairs or small groups, using the Powers of Ten materials to carry out similar examples. One child in each group should record the algorithm as the action is taking place. Include examples with 0 in the dividend and in the quotient, as well as some that have a remainder.

EXTENSION: Use tiles and /or dollars, dimes and pennies.

Activity 43: Division with 4-Digit Numbers

MATERIALS: Powers of Ten Blocks and Cups.

Write 3 1641 on the chalkboard. Ask children what is needed to carry out the example with materials. Proceed as in Activity 42 above.

Activity 44: Dividing Multiples of Tens, Hundreds and Thousands by a One-Digit Number

MATERIALS: Powers of Ten Blocks and Cups.

Record on the chalkboard as children carry out the following examples with materials. 6 ÷ 6, 60 ÷ 6, 600 ÷ 6. Ask what the quotient will be for 6,000 ÷ 6 (1,000), 60,000 ÷ 6 (10,000), 600,000 ÷ 6, (100,000). Continue similarly for 4 ÷ 4, 40 ÷ 4, 400 ÷ 4, etc.; repeat for 12 ÷ 3, 120 ÷ 3, 1,200 ÷ 3, etc. Have children formulate a "rule" for this pattern.

Activity 45: Divisibility by 2, 5, and 10

MATERIALS: Powers of Ten Blocks, Cups, Master 9.

Divide the class into 4 or 5 groups. Discuss the meaning of divisibility in general and divisibility by 2 in particular. Orally, have the children solve 20 ÷ 2, 18 ÷ 2, . . . 2 ÷ 2. On Master 9, have children circle the numbers that are divisible by 2 from 2-20. Assign several of the following examples for each group to solve using Powers of Ten materials, recording the answers on the chalkboard: 32 ÷ 2, 38 ÷ 2, 24 ÷ 2, 13 ÷ 2, 40 ÷ 2, 31 ÷ 2, 25 ÷ 2, 36 ÷ 2, 27 ÷ 2, 19 ÷ 2. On Master 9, have children circle additional numbers they found to be divisible by 2. Have them look at the chart and predict whether 76 is divisible by 2, then prove it with the Powers of Ten materials. Encourage children to generalize a rule for divisibility by 2: A number is divisible by 2 if its last digit is divisible by 2 (i.e. 0, 2, 4, ... 8.) Ask if 356 is divisible by 2 and why.

Follow similar procedures to develop a rule for divisibility by 5 on Master 9. Have children "triangle" the numbers they find to be divisible by 5: A number is divisible by 5 if its last digit is a 5 or a 0.

Ask which numbers are circled and "triangled" on Master 9, and record on the chalkboard (10, 20, 30, ... 100). Ask children to find another number that can divide all the numbers listed (10), and generalize the rule for divisibility by 10. (A number is divisible by 10 if its last digit is 0).

91	92	93	94	95	96	97	98	99	100
81	82	83	84	85	86	87	88	89	90
71	72	73	74	75	76	77	78	79	80
61	62	63	64	65	66	67	68	69	70
51	52	53	54	55	56	57	58	59	60
41	42	43	44	45	46	47	48	49	50
31	32	33	34	35	36	37	38	39	40
21	22	23	24	25	26	27	28	29	30
11	(12)	13	(14)	△15	(16)	17	(18)	19	△(20)
1	(2)	3	(4)	△5	(6)	7	(8)	9	△(10)

MATERIALS: Powers of Ten Blocks, Cups, Master 9.

Repeat Activity 45 to develop divisibility by 3, having children draw a square on those numbers on Master 9 that are divisible by 3. Ask if a rule for divisibility by 3 can be developed by looking at the last digit of a number as was done for divisibility by 2, 5, and 10 (No). On the chalkboard, list one column of numbers that are divisible by 3 and another column of numbers that are not. Have children add the digits of each number on both lists. Discuss the results and generalize that a number is divisible by 3 if the sum of its digits is divisible by 3.

MATERIALS: Powers of Ten Blocks, Tiles, Money, Cups.

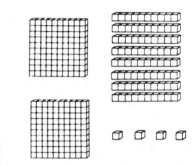

Review rounding to the nearest ten or hundred as in Activity 14. Write 28 ÷ 6 on the chalkboard. Have children round 28 to the nearest ten (i.e. 30), and write the rounded example on the chalkboard (30 ÷ 6). Display it with Powers of Ten materials, divide the materials into 6 cups, and record the quotient. Then have children display the actual amount, divide, and record. Compare the nearness of the 2 quotients. Repeat with other 2 digit division examples.

Write 584 ÷ 32 on the chalkboard. Discuss the need for rounding both the divisor and dividend to 1 significant digit. Have children round 584 to the nearest hundred and display 600. Round 32 to the nearest ten (30). Write the rounded example on the chalkoard (600 ÷ 30). Review division by multiples of 10, having children tell how many tens equal 600 (60). Trade to prove it.

Write 1,894 ÷ 46 on the chalkboard. Repeat the rounding discussion and write the rounded example on the chalkboard (2,000 ÷ 50). Have children display 2,000 using Powers of Ten materials. Ask how many 100's in 2,000 (20), 10's in 2,000 (200), 50's or 5 tens in 2,000 (40). Have children display the example with the materials. Repeat for 1,894 ÷ 465, etc.

EXTENSIONS: Use tiles and/or money, following similar procedures.

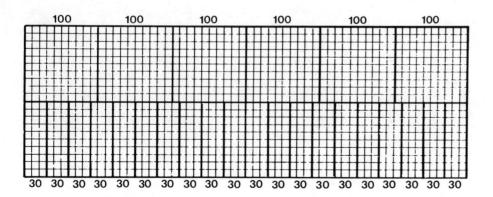

$$600 \div 30 = 20$$

$$20 \times 30 = 600$$

INTRODUCTION TO ALGEBRA
(MULTIPLICATION AND DIVISION)

Activities 48-49

Activity 48: Introduction to Algebra: Multiplication Number Sentences   4 5 6 7 8

MATERIALS: Tiles and Envelopes.

"Secretly" place 3 tiles into each of four envelopes and display the envelopes. Tell children there are 12 tiles altogether. Record on the chalkboard: 4 envelopes = 12 tiles. Ask children to decide how many tiles are in each envelope (3), and tell the operation used to solve (division). Empty each envelope to show the four groups of 3. Rewrite the number sentence for the action using "n" for the unknown number of tiles instead of "envelopes": 4n = 12. Write the division sentence used to solve: n = 12 ÷ 4. Repeat the procedure several times with different numbers.

Play "The Missing Number" game. Distribute 5 envelopes and 20 tiles to each pair of children. Player 1 sets up a number sentence as above using as many envelopes and tiles as s/he wishes, and writes the appropriate number sentence. Player 2 writes the related division sentence, solves for n and checks by emptying the envelopes. In the next round, roles are reversed. Player 1 receives one point for the correct "set up" and 1 point for writing the appropriate number sentence. Player 2 receives 1 point for writing the related number sentence and 1 point for correctly solving the problem. Play continues until one player has attained 10 points.

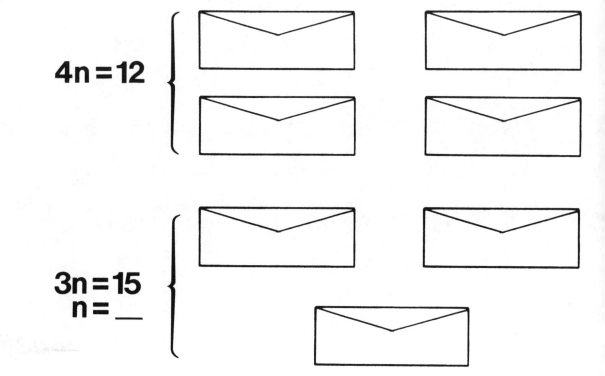

$4n = 12$

$3n = 15$
$n = \underline{\hspace{1cm}}$

MATERIALS: Tiles and Envelopes.

"Secretly" place 15 tiles into an envelope. Tell children that the tiles can be removed from the envelope and stacked into 3 piles, with 5 tiles in each. Record on the chalkboard: Envelope ÷ 5 = 3. Ask children to decide how many tiles are in the envelope (15), and tell the operation they used to solve (multiplication). Remove the tiles from the envelope and stack them in the appropriate piles. Rewrite the number sentence for the action using "n" for the unknown number of tiles instead of "envelope": n ÷ 5 = 3. Write the related number sentence: n = 3 x 5. Repeat with different numbers.

Play "The Missing Numbers" game. Follow the directions given in Activity 48.

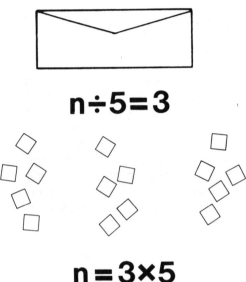

$$n \div 5 = 3$$

$$n = 3 \times 5$$

FRACTIONS AND MIXED NUMBERS

Activities 50-74

Activity 50: Introducing Fraction Concepts

4 5 6 7 8

MATERIALS: Fraction Circle Set, Masters 10-12, Scissors, Envelopes.

Have children locate the whole circles on Masters 10-12. Label them "1 or 1 whole" and cut them out. Display the two halves, from the Fraction Circle Set. Have children identify them, explain what half means, (1 of 2 equal parts), and find the matching pieces on Master 10. Color to match the plastic set if desired, label each 1/2, and cut them out. Review the meaning of the symbol 1/2 (1 means the one piece we have; 2 means that the whole was cut into 2 equal pieces). Introduce the terms numerator and denominator. Repeat the activity for thirds and fourths on Master 10, sixths and eighths on Master 11, fifths and tenths on Master 12. Have children display other fractions (i.e., 2/3, 6/8, 4/6, 1/10, etc.). On the chalkboard, record the symbol for each fraction displayed, relating the symbol to the actual pieces. Reiterate the meaning of numerator and denominator. Children should store the circles in an envelope.

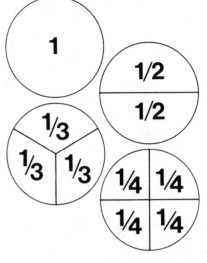

Activity 51: Fractional Names for Whole Numbers

4 5 6 7 8

MATERIALS: Fraction Circles Set, Fraction Masters 10-12, Scissors, Envelopes.

Take the unit circles from Masters 10-12, and have children cover them in as many different ways as possible with fraction pieces of ONE COLOR. Record the results on a chalkboard chart. Have children observe the patterns to generalize the rule for fractional names for 1: The numerator and the denominator are the same numeral. Introduce the fraction symbol for 1 whole as 1/1, having the children use the circles to explain it.

EXTENSION: Have children work in groups of 4, sharing the fraction circles, to find fractional names for 2, 3, 4.

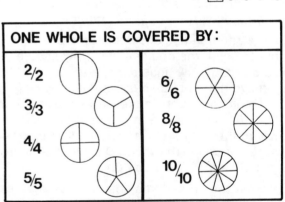

ONE WHOLE IS COVERED BY:

2/2   6/6

3/3   8/8

4/4   10/10

5/5

Activity 52: Developing a Fraction Line

4 5 6 7 8

MATERIALS: Fraction Circles Set, Masters 10-12.

Have children build a "Fraction Line" using the fraction pieces cut from Masters 10-12. Children should take one of each fraction piece and order the pieces from largest to smallest. Tape the Fraction Line to the chalkboard and record using fraction symbols and fraction pieces. Review how many pieces of each fraction are needed to form 1, relating the number of pieces needed to the denominator of the fraction. Point out the inverse relationship between the denominator and the actual size of each fraction part. Discuss other fractions such as 1/9 and 1/7, deciding where to place them.

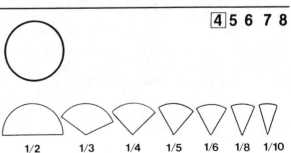

1/2   1/3   1/4   1/5   1/6   1/8   1/10

Activity 53: Equal (Equivalent) Fractions

MATERIALS: Fraction Circles Set, Masters 10-12.

Display the 1/2 piece from the Fraction Circle Set. Have children match it with a paper piece, and find as many ways as possible to cover it with other pieces of ONE COLOR or ONE SIZE. Record each discovery on a chalkboard chart called "Other Names for 1/2". Have children observe the patterns on the chart to develop a generalization for deriving equivalent fractions. (The denominator is twice the numerator or the numerator is one half the denominator.) Repeat the activity for thirds, fourths, sixths, eighths, fifths and tenths.

EXTENSION: Play "Find One to Match" to reinforce these discoveries. Children play in pairs using the paper circles. The first child displays a set of fractional parts on a unit circle. (i.e. 6/8). The second child must match it with at least one equivalent fraction and scores one point for each equivalent fraction displayed. Roles reverse after each turn. The first player to reach 10 points wins.

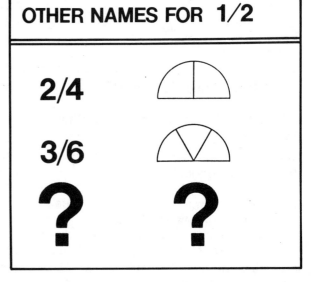

Activity 54: Fractions On A Number Line

MATERIALS: Tiles, Master 13.

Have children use equal amounts of tiles, of two different colors to cover the number line on Master 13. Have them arrange the tiles by color, draw a line to separate the two colors, and remove the tiles. Discuss the number of parts formed, and compare each part to the whole. Have children mark the center line 1/2. Review the meaning of this demarcation. Discuss the meaning of 0/2 and 2/2 and decide where these symbols should be written on the number line.

Have children use equal amounts of tiles of four different colors to cover the number line. They should arrange the tiles by color, then draw lines to separate each of the four colors and remove the tiles. Discuss the number of parts formed, and compare each part to the whole. Have children mark the first line 1/4. Discuss the meaning of 2/4, 3/4, 4/4, and 0/4. Decide where these symbols should be written on the number line and have children write them. Discuss the equivalence of 1/2 and 2/4; 2/2 and 4/4; 0/2 and 0/4.

Repeat the procedures described using tiles of three different colors to locate thirds on the number line. Use 12 tiles of one color and introduce twelfths. Discuss the equivalence of 1/3, 3/12; 1/2, 2/4, 6/12; etc.

EXTENSION: Discuss how to show sixths on the number line. Have children use tiles to demonstrate the location of each sixth, and then write the symbols in the appropriate places. Discuss the equivalence of sixths, halves, thirds, etc.

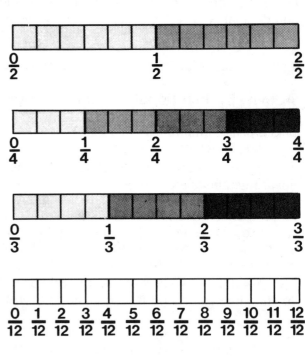

Activity 55: Identifying Fractions of a Set

MATERIALS: Tiles, Coins.

Have children display a set of 8 tiles containing 3 red and 5 green. Identify the total number of tiles in the set and the number of tiles that are red. Record on the chalkboard as 3 (red tiles) out of 8 (tiles in the set) or 3/8. Review the information given by the numerator and denominator. Ask children to write a fraction that shows the number of green tiles in the set. Continue using different combinations of tiles in 2 colors, having children display the set, determine the total number of tiles, and record the fraction of the set for each color. Repeat the activity with tiles of three colors. Do the same, using coins of different denominations.

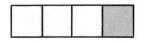

EXTENSION: Pose problems: "A set contains 4 tiles. 3/4 of the set is blue. The rest of the set is green. How many tiles are green?" Have children display the problem with tiles and explain how to arrive at the solution.

Activity 56: Fractions of a Number

4 5 6 7 8

MATERIALS: Tiles, Unit Cubes, Coins.

Have children display 16 tiles. Find 1/2 of the set and prove it. Record as 1/2 of 16 = □. Discuss the various proofs the children offer and record the answer 8 . Continue finding 1/2 of various numbers by having the children display each number as a set of objects using any of the above materials. Record each example and answer on the chalkboard. Look for patterns to develop a generalization about finding 1/2 of a number. Repeat the Activity similarly to find 1/4, 1/3, 1/6, 1/8 of a number, and develop an overall generalization about finding a fraction of a number.

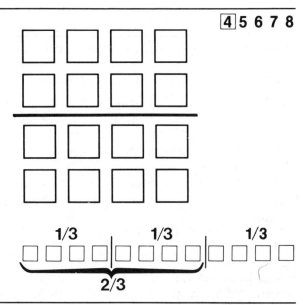

EXTENSION: After finding 1/3 of 12, challenge the children to find 2/3 of 12, demonstrating their solution with materials. Repeat with other non-unit fractions.

Activity 57: Recognizing Mixed Numbers

4 5 6 7 8

MATERIALS: Fraction Circles Set, Masters 10-12.

Children should work in pairs to share the fraction circles made from Masters 10-12. Have them display 4 thirds and find how many unit circles (wholes) these pieces will cover. How many thirds are left? Record on the chalkboard as 4 thirds or $4/3 = 1\frac{1}{3}$. Continue similarly, simplifying fractions such as 6/4, 7/3, 9/5, 12/8 etc.

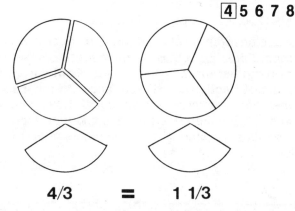

4/3   =   1 1/3

EXTENSION: Have children reverse the above action, displaying the mixed number first and converting it into the fraction (i.e. 2 ½ is how many halves? etc.).

Activity 58: Renaming Fractions

4 5 6 7 8

MATERIALS: Fraction Circle Set, Masters 10-12.

Review the different fractional names for 1 (Activity 51) and have children display these with fraction circle pieces. Record on a chalkboard chart. Have children display 3 unit circles. Record on the chart as 3 and ask them to "rename" one of the circles by covering it with thirds. Discuss the name and value of the "covered" circle. Record on the chart as $2\frac{3}{3}$. Compare the materials displayed to the original 3 circles. Remove the thirds and repeat the activity, covering one of the circles with fourths. Continue similarly using sixths, halves, fifths, eighths and tenths. Discuss the chart and develop a generalization.

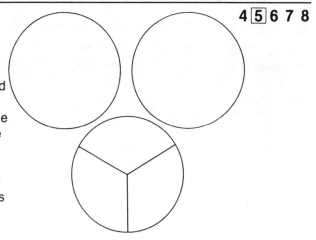

Activity 59: Simplifying Fractions: Greatest Common Factor

MATERIALS: Tiles.

Use tiles to review factoring and finding common factors of 2 or 3 numbers (see Activities 33-34). Introduce the term "Greatest Common Factor" (GCF). Discuss its meaning, relating it to the common factors already found. Have children find the GCF of 5 and 10, 3 and 6, 4 and 8, etc. using tiles. Discuss simplifying fractions, i.e. to simplify 4/8, divide the numerator and the denominator by their GCF. Have children simplify fractions using the GCF.

Activity 60: Comparing Unit Fractions

MATERIALS: Fraction Circles Set, Masters 10-13.

Develop a "Fraction Line" as in Activity 52. Discuss the relative size of the pieces. Review the > and < symbols. Have children use the "Fraction Line" and the fraction circles to compare unit fractions. Use the symbols > and < to record (i.e. 1/2 > 1/8).

EXTENSION: Use the Fraction Number Lines (developed in Activity 54) to compare fractions. Use inequalities (> and <) to record.

Activity 61: Comparing Fractions and/or Mixed Numbers

MATERIALS: Fraction Circles Set, Masters 10-12.

Have children display 2/3 and 3/8, decide which is larger, and record as 2/3 > 3/8. Have them place one set of pieces on top of the other to verify the answer. Continue comparing other pairs of fractions, and recording with the inequality symbols. Include some pairs that are equal. Have children display 1 2/3 and 4/3, compare the displays and then record with symbols. Continue comparing mixed numbers and/or fractions.

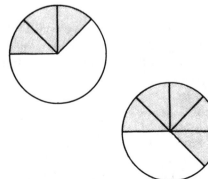

2/3 > 3/8

Activity 62: Addition of Fractions With Common Denominators

MATERIALS: Fraction Circles Set, Masters 10-12, Tiles.

Using the unit circle as a base, have children display three 1/8 pieces. Ask how many in all and record 3/8. Have them add two 1/8 pieces to the display and record as 2/8. Have them find the total. Record as 5/8; or 3/8 + 2/8 = 5/8. Continue similarly, with children displaying pairs of fractions with the same denominators, and then combining to find the sum.

EXTENSION: Repeat the activity using mixed numbers. Have children close their eyes and take a handful of tiles. Have them count the total number of tiles in the set, and the number of tiles of each color. Write a fraction addition sentence to describe the set of tiles.

Activity 63: Subtraction of Fractions With Common Denominators: "Take Away" Model

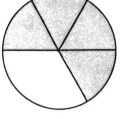
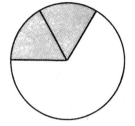

MATERIALS: Fraction Circles Set, Masters 10-12.

Using the unit circle as a base, have children display 4/6. Then take away 2/6 and tell how many sixths are left. Record on the chalkboard in horizontal and vertical notation. Continue similarly with a variety of examples involving subtraction with common denominators.

EXTENSION: Repeat the Activity with mixed numbers.

Activity 64: Addition of Fractions With Different Denominators

MATERIALS: Fraction Circles Set, Masters 10-12, Unit Cubes.

Using the unit circle as a base, have children display 1/2 with the fraction circle pieces. Ask them to find other ways to cover the half with one color or size. Record each combination as an addition sentence (i.e. 1/4 + 1/4 = 1/2; 1/6 + 1/6 + 1/6 = 1/2, etc.). Repeat the activity, having them find pieces of 2 different colors or sizes to cover the half. Record the combinations as addition sentences (i.e. 1/4 + 2/8 = 1/2; 1/3 + 1/6 = 1/2, etc.). Discuss the two sets of addition sentences, comparing the terms to find similarities or differences (i.e. with 1/4 + 1/4 = 1/2 and 1/4 + 2/8 = 1/2, children should be led to notice that 1/4 and 2/8 are equivalent fractions).

Have children use the fraction circle pieces to solve examples involving addition with different denominators such as 1/3 + 1/2. Have children find pieces of one color or one size that cover both (sixths). As each example is solved with the pieces, have children explain their actions and record on the chalkboard using vertical notation.

EXTENSION: Play "Circle Cover-Up" using the fraction circle pieces and 1 unit cube labeled 1/2, 1/3, 1/4, 1/6, 1/8, 1/8. A second cube may be made and used instead, labeled 1/2, 1/5, 1/5, 1/10, 1/10. A unit circle is the gameboard. The goal is to completely cover the unit circle with fractional parts. Children roll the cube, read aloud the fraction that is rolled, pick up a piece that size and place it on the gameboard. At all times THE PIECES ON THE GAMEBOARD MUST BE OF THE SAME COLOR. If necessary, exchanges for equivalent fraction pieces may be made before a turn is finished. The first player to cover the unit circle exactly wins.

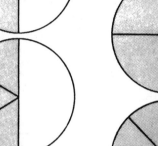
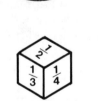

Activity 65: Subtraction of Fractions with Common Denominators: "Missing Addend Model"

MATERIALS: Fraction Circles Set, Masters 10-12.

Using the unit circle on Master 10, display 5/8 with the plastic pieces. On top of the 5/8, place 2/8 and ask how many more eighths are needed to make 5/8. Record as a missing addend sentence: 5/8 = 2/8 + □. Develop and record the related subtraction sentence 5/8 − 2/8 = □.

Repeat the activity several times using fractions with common denominators, having children display the example, solve and

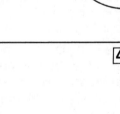

record it as a missing addend sentence and a related subtraction sentence.

EXTENSION: Repeat the activity using fractions that do not have common denominators, e.g. 1/2 − 1/3.

Activity 66: Subtraction of Fractions With Different Denominators

MATERIALS: Fraction Circles Set, Masters 10-12.

Write 3/4 − 5/8 on the chalkboard. Have children display three-fourths. Discuss how to take 5/8 away. Have children use the fraction circle pieces to rename 3/4 as an equivalent fraction in eighths. Once 3/4 has been renamedband displayed as 6/8, have children complete the example. Record the actions on the chalkboard. Repeat the activity several times. Include examples with mixed numbers. For examples like 2/3 − 1/2, both fractions will have to be renamed.

EXTENSION: Write on the chalkboard $2\frac{1}{8}$ − 3/8. Have children display $2\frac{1}{8}$ and discuss how 3/8 may be subtracted. (A review of Activity 58 may be needed.) After renaming 2 as 1 and 8/8, combine the 8/8 and 1/8 to make 9/8. They will now have $1\frac{9}{8}$ displayed. Record the actions with materials on the chalkboard, using fraction symbols, so that the recording is an exact parallel. Have children take away 3/8 to solve. Repeat several times for similar examples.

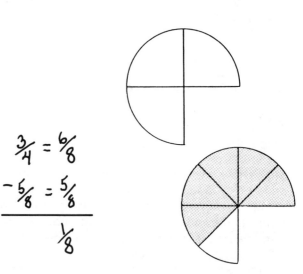

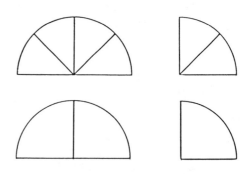

Activity 67: Introducing Least Common Denominator

MATERIALS: Fraction Circles Set, Masters 10-12.

Have children display the 1/4 and 1/2 pieces and cover each with eighths. Ask them to name the resulting equivalent fractions, emphasizing the common denominator, eighths. Have them cover the 1/2 and the 1/4 pieces with fourths to find equivalent fractions with a common denominator. Ask which pair of equivalent fractions, eighths or fourths, uses fewer pieces (fourths). Introduce the term "least common denominator". Repeat the activity for 3/4 and 1/2, 2/3 and 1/2, 2/5 and 1/2, etc.

Activity 68: Multiplication of Fractions: (Whole Number Times a Fraction)

MATERIALS: Fraction Circles Set, Masters 10-12.

Have children display 3 of the 1/8 pieces, then combine the pieces to find the total. Record as 1/8 + 1/8 + 1/8 = 3/8. Relate the repeated addition example to multiplication and rewrite as: 3 x 1/8 = 3/8. Repeat for examples such as 2 x 1/4.

EXTENSION: Have children display 4 sets of 2/4. Write the repeated addition and the multiplication examples on the chalkboard. Have them combine the fourths to find the product, forming as many whole circles as possible in the process. While 8/4 describes the number of pieces accurately, children should be encouraged to rename the pieces in terms of a whole number or a mixed number. Repeat for examples like 4 x 3/8.

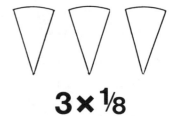

$3 \times \frac{1}{8}$

Activity 69: Multiplication of Fractions: Fraction Times Whole Number

MATERIALS: Fraction Circles Set, Tiles, Masters 10-12.

Have children display a set of 2 unit circles and find 1/2 of the set. Show 3 unit circles and find 2/3 of them. Show 4 unit circles and find 1/4 of them, then 2/4, and 3/4. Record on the chalkboard as 1/2 x 2 = 1, 2/3 x 3 = 2, etc. Introduce the word "of" for the x symbol. Repeat the activity for other examples.

EXTENSION: Repeat the activity with tiles. Pose problems such as a set contains 6 tiles. 5/6 of the tiles are red. How many tiles are red?

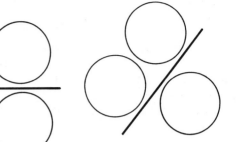

Activity 70: Multiplications of Fractions: Fraction Times Fraction

MATERIALS: Fraction Circles Set, Masters 10-12, Scissors.

Have children display a 1/3 piece and find half of it. Discuss how this may be accomplished (i.e. folding or cutting the third) and have them do it. After finding half of a 1/3 piece, have them locate the fraction circle piece that matches it (1/6), and prove it by covering. Record on a chalkboard chart: 1/2 of 1/3 = 1/6. Continue, having children use the fraction circle pieces to solve examples such as, 1/2 x 1/4, 1/2 x 1/5, etc. Record each solution on the chalkboard chart and have children look for a pattern across each row to discover the rule for multiplication of fractions.

EXTENSION: Have children display 6/8 and then find 1/2 of it. Encourage them to think of 6/8 as six 1/8 pieces and then simply find half of the set (or three 1/8 pieces). Record as 1/2 x 6/8 = 3/8. Then have children solve the example by following the rule discovered for multiplication of fractions. Discuss whether the 2 products 6/16 and 3/8 are the same.

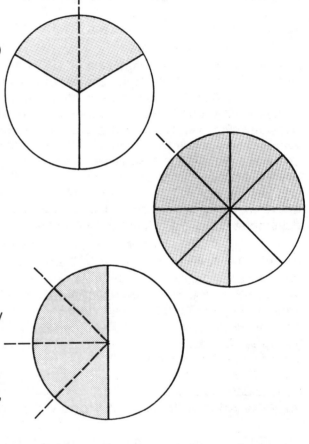

Have children display the 1/2 piece and then find 2/4 of it. Discuss methods for solving the example and have children try them out. The 1/2 piece may be folded into four equal parts and 2/4 colored or cut out. Match this part with the fraction pieces to find that it is equivalent to 1/4 of the whole circle. Record as 2/4 x 1/2 = 1/4. Does this example follow the rule for multiplication of fractions? Repeat with 2/3 x 1/2, 3/4 x 1/2, 4/5 x 1/2, etc.

Activity 71: Introduction to Division of Fractions

MATERIALS: Fraction Circles Set, Masters 10-12.

Review the meaning of division as repeated subtraction. (See Activity 40.) Refer to this interpretation in the following Activity. Have children display 1/2. Ask them to cover the half with sixths. How many sixths are needed? Record as 3 sixths are in 1/2. Continue, finding the number of eighths and tenths in 1/2 and recording similarly. Discuss each of the actions and relate it to the division process. Next to each recorded result, write the appropriate division sentence, e.g., for 3 sixths are in 1/2, write 1/2 ÷ 1/6 = 3. Ask children to explain why the answer is sometimes a whole number when fractions are divided. They should refer to the action, i.e., the 3 refers to 3 sixths. Repeat for various examples such as 1/3 ÷ 1/6, 3/4 ÷ 1/8, etc.

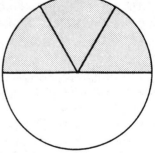

Activity 72: Division of Fractions With Mixed Numbers

MATERIALS: Fraction Circles Set, Masters 10-12.

Have children display 5 thirds. Ask them to show one set of 2 thirds and then find how many sets of 2/3 are in 5/3. They should be able to show that 2 full sets of 2/3 can be formed and 1/2 of a set is left over. Record the action as $5/3 \div 2/3 = 2\frac{1}{2}$. Continue similarly with examples such as $7/8 \div 2/8$; $6/5 \div 4/5$.

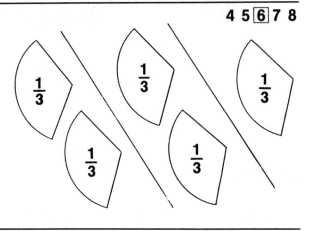

Activity 73: Division of Fractions With Common Denominators

MATERIALS: Fraction Circles Set, Masters 10-12.

Have children display 6 tenths. Ask them to show one set of 2/10 and then find how many sets of 2/10 are in 6/10. Record as $6/10 \div 2/10 = 3$. Continue similarly for such examples as $6/8 \div 3/8$, $8/6 \div 2/6$, etc. Have children look for a pattern across the rows and discuss their observations. Elicit the generalization that if two fractions have common denominators we need only divide the numerators to find a solution. Have children use this rule to solve examples like $6/10 \div 3/10$, $8/6 \div 2/6$, and then check using the fraction circles. Ask how the rule can be applied to solve $1/2 \div 1/4$. The examples can be rewritten, using equivalent fractions to get a common denominator i.e., $2/4 \div 1/4$, then solved (2).

$$\frac{6}{10} \div \frac{2}{10} = 3$$

Have children display 3/5. Ask them to show one set of 2/10 and then find how many sets of 2/10 are in 3/5. Record as $3/5 \div 2/10 = 3$ sets. Continue similarly with examples such as $3/4 \div 2/8$, $3/2 \div 2/4$; $2/3 \div 4/6$, etc. Apply the common denominator rule to check each problem.

$$\frac{6}{8} \div \frac{3}{8} = 2$$

Activity 74: Division of Fractions With Different Denominators

MATERIALS: Fraction Circles Set, Masters 10-12.

Have children display 1/2. Ask them to find how many thirds are in 1/2. Discuss possible solutions and have children use the fraction pieces to try each. One solution is to place the 1/3 piece on top of 1/2; extra space will remain. Children should find the fraction piece that covers this space (1/6). Ask "What part is the 1/6 piece of the 1/3 piece?" (half of it). This means there is one 1/3 piece and 1/2 of another in 1/2 ($1/2 \div 1/3 = 1\frac{1}{2}$).

A second approach is to find equivalent fractions for 1/2 and 1/3 that have a common denominator. The problem now is simplified and children can see that $3/6 \div 2/6 = 1$ set of 2/6 and 1 extra 1/6 piece (or 1/2 of the set) so $1/2 \div 1/3 = 1\frac{1}{2}$. The common denominator approach can be used to check. (See Activity 73). Many examples of this type should be done to ensure that children understand the seemingly odd answers that appear, such as $5/6 \div 1/2 = 1\frac{2}{3}$, $4/5 \div 3/10 = 2\frac{2}{3}$, etc.

$$\frac{1}{2} = \frac{3}{6}$$
$$\frac{1}{3} = \frac{2}{6}$$

RATIOS AND PROPORTIONS

Activities 75-77

Activity 75: Ratios

4 5 6 7 8

MATERIALS: Tiles, Money.

Have children display 3 red and 4 green tiles. Describe the display by saying there are 4 green tiles for every 3 red tiles. This is called a ratio. Record on the chalkboard as: 3 red to 4 green; 3 to 4; 3:4 or 3/4. Have children display various combinations of tiles using 2 colors. Record the ratios for each on the chalkboard. Write "5 to 2" on the chalkboard, have children display it with tiles and then tell how to write other forms of the ratio. Continue, writing one form of a ratio on the chalkboard and proceeding as above. Ask if 2:3 is the same as 3:2? (No) Have children use materials to demonstrate their answers.

EXTENSION: Have children display 5 tiles and 3 pennies and tell the ratio. (5 tiles to 3¢). Record on the chalkboard. Explain that this can be interpreted as buying "5 tiles for 3¢". Repeat with similar "pricing" activities.

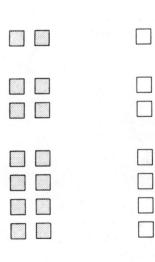

Activity 76: Equivalent Ratios

4 5 6 7 8

MATERIALS: Tiles, Money.

Have children display 2 blue tiles and 1 green tile and tell you the ratio (2:1). Record on the chalkboard. Write "4 to 2" and "8 to 4" on the chalkboard. Have children display each using blue tiles for the larger amount and green tiles for the smaller one. Discuss and demonstrate the relationship among the three ratios: they are the same since for every 2 blue tiles, there is 1 green tile. Write "3:4" on the chalkboard. Have children display two equivalent ratios using tiles, then record. Repeat for other ratios.

EXTENSION: Have children display equivalent ratios using tiles and coins. i.e. 4 tiles for 5¢; 8 tiles for 10¢. Discuss the equivalence of the two "prices".

MATERIALS: Tiles, Money.

Write "2:3" on the chalkboard and have children display the ratio with red and yellow tiles. Describe the display (2 red tiles to 3 yellow). Have children show an equivalent ratio, using 8 red tiles. Ask how many yellow tiles will be needed (12), and discuss methods of solving the problem. Repeat with other examples. Alternate, having children find the first or the second numeral in the proportion. Write "3/4 = ?/16" on the chalkboard. Discuss the meaning of the proportion and have children solve it using tiles. Repeat for several other proportions, varying the position of the ?

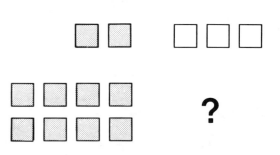

EXTENSION: Display 3 tiles and 1 dime. Ask children to interpret the display, and ask how many tiles could be purchased for 50¢? (15) Have children use tiles and dimes to prove their answers. Ask how much 6 tiles would cost (20¢), again having them use materials to prove the answers. Repeat with similar examples.

DECIMALS AND PERCENT

Activities 78-91

Activity 78: Introducing Tenths

MATERIALS: Powers of Ten Blocks, Cuisenaire Place Value Chart, and Master 12.
LET ORANGE ROD = 1 WHOLE

Have children find how many white cubes are equivalent to the orange rod (10). What part of the orange rod is one white cube (1/10)? Have children display 3/10, 7/10, 1 $\frac{4}{10}$, etc. Ask them to display 23 $\frac{2}{10}$. Have children display other mixed numbers using tenths, recording the appropriate numerals on the chalkboard. Discuss the display of 23 $\frac{2}{10}$, asking how to show 23 if the orange rod is one (23 orange rods or 2 flats and 3 rods). Use Powers of Ten materials at the top of each column on the Cuisenaire Place Value Chart. Display 23 $\frac{2}{10}$ on the Chart if the orange rod is one. Ask the value of the blocks in the column headed by the white cube.

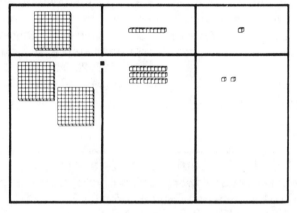

Write 23 $\frac{2}{10}$ and 23.2 on the chalkboard. Explain that by convention, we use a dot or decimal point as another way to represent a fractional number. Refer to the Cuisenaire Place Value Chart, and ask children where to place the decimal point to separate the fraction from the whole number. Explain that the numeral now reads 23 and two tenths, and can be written with the decimal point (23.2) or as a mixed numeral (23 $\frac{2}{10}$). Have children tell you how to rewrite the numerals previously recorded on the chalkboard as decimals. Write 8.3 on the chalkboard. Have children display it with their materials and read it (eight and 3 tenths). Repeat for several other numerals.

VARIATION: Use Master 12. Repeat or review the development of tenths using the fraction circles.

Activity 79: Introducing Hundredths

MATERIALS: Powers of Ten Blocks, Cuisenaire Place Value Chart, Masters 14 and 15.
LET ORANGE FLAT = 1 WHOLE

Assign a value of 1 to the flat. Have children use the Powers of **Ten** materials and explain the value of the orange rod (1/10 and the unit cube (1/100). Write 0.1 and 0.01 on the chalkboard, and **ask** where to place the decimal point on the Cuisenaire Place Value Chart when the flat is one. Have children display 3/100, 2 $\frac{3}{10}$, 2 $\frac{33}{100}$ on the Chart. Using Master 14, relate the outlined grids to the flat. Explain that if the flat is one, then each small square is 1/100. Have children color in 33/100 on the first outline, and then cover the enclosed area with white cubes and orange rods. Explain that 33/100 is equal to 3/10 plus 3/100, or 0.3 plus 0.03.

Write 1.12 and 1 $\frac{12}{100}$ on the chalkboard. Have children display it on the Cuisenaire Place Value Chart, and show you where to place the decimal point. Draw the Chart on the chalkboard and

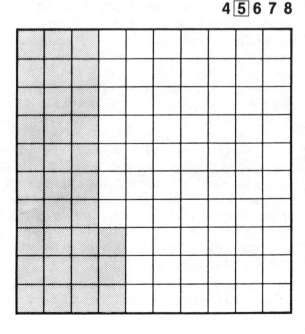

record the children's display using numerals. Continue, having children display decimal fractions or mixed numbers with Powers of Ten materials on the Chart, and recording the numerals on the chalkboard diagram. Have children record the numeral for each decimal fraction colored on Master 14 in the space provided. Include numbers like $3\frac{10}{100}$, $3\frac{1}{100}$, and 4/100. Write 3.25 on the chalkboard. Have children display it with materials on the Chart, then color only the decimal fraction portion on Master 14. Repeat for other numbers, including several like 3.20 and 3.02.

EXTENSION: Complete Master 15.

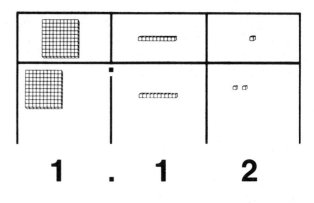

Activity 80: Introducing Thousandths

MATERIALS: Powers of Ten Blocks, Cuisenaire Place Value Chart, Masters 16 and 17.
LET ORANGE CUBE = 1 WHOLE

Assign a value of 1 to the orange cube. Have children use the Powers of Ten materials, and explain the values of the flat (1/10), the orange rod (1/100), and the unit cube (1/1000). Draw a diagram of the Place Value Chart on the chalkboard. Write 0.1, 0.01, and 0.001, and ask where to place the decimal point on the Cuisenaire Place Value Chart. Explain that since the Chart has only 3 columns, the orange cube will be placed to the left of the mat to show whole numbers. Follow the procedures described in Activities 78 and 79, having children display mixed numbers and decimal fractions using thousandths. Include numbers like $2\frac{102}{1000}$, $2\frac{12}{1000}$, 2.013, 2.004, etc.

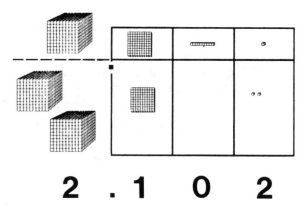

EXTENSION: Have children display decimal fractions using thousandths, and record the numerals on Master 16. Complete Master 17.

Activity 81: Equivalent Decimals

MATERIALS: Powers of Ten Blocks, Cuisenaire Place Value Chart, Dimes and Pennies, Master 2.
LET ORANGE CUBE = 1 WHOLE

Assign a value of 1 to the orange cube. Review the values of the other Powers of Ten pieces (Flat: 1/10, 0.1; orange rod: 1/100, 0.01, unit cube: 1/1000, 0.001). Have children display 0.2 on the Cuisenaire Place Value Chart. Discuss which Powers of Ten pieces were used (2 flats) and why. Record 0.2 on the chalkboard. Ask children to tell the value of one orange rod (1/100), and how many orange rods could be traded for one flat (10). Have them trade the flats for orange rods and tell the value of the display (0.20). Record on the chalkboard writing 0.2 = 0.20. Ask for the value of one unit cube (1/1000) and how many unit cubes could be traded for one orange rod (10); for two orange rods (20); for 10 orange rods (100); for 20 orange rods (200). Ask what value the 200 unit cubes would have (200 thousandths). On the chalkboard continue the equality sentence writing 0.200 after 0.20. Develop other decimal equivalents, such as 0.6, 0.60, 0.600 similarly, recording on the chalkboard as a chart. Discuss the pattern to develop a generalization about equivalent decimals.

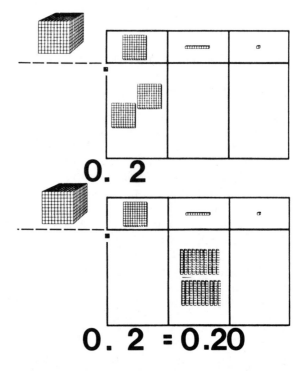

Discuss money, eliciting that 1 dime is 0.1 dollar and a penny is 0.01 dollar. Use dimes and pennies on Master 2 to show the equivalence of $0.3 and $0.30, etc.

EXTENSION: Write 0.18 on the chalkboard. Have children display it with Powers of Ten materials on the Cuisenaire Place Value Chart, then trade to show an equivalent form (0.180). Include decimals such as 0.04.

Activity 82: Expanded Notation

MATERIALS: Powers of Ten Blocks, Cuisenaire Place Value Chart, and Master 16.
LET ORANGE CUBE = 1 WHOLE

Write 2.453 on the chalkboard. Have children display it on the Cuisenaire Place Value Chart, using Powers of Ten materials. Have them read the display and write the expanded numeral. Repeat several times. Include numerals which have zeroes in various places.

Write several expanded numerals on the chalkboard. Have children display each, then write the standard numeral. Include numerals with zeroes in various places. Write 3.5̲49 on the chalkboard. Have children display only the underlined digit in the appropriate column on Master 2, and then read the display. (Children should display 4 orange rods in the hundredths column and read it as 4 hundredths or 40 thousandths.) Repeat for other numerals, having children record each display on Master 16.

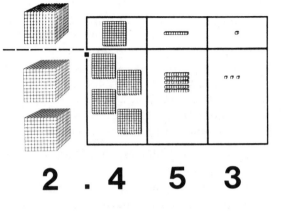

2 . 4   5   3

Activity 83: Comparing Decimals

MATERIALS: Powers of Ten Blocks, Cuisenaire Place Value Chart, and Master 2.
LET ORANGE CUBE = 1 WHOLE

On the chalkboard, write 0.6 and 0.8. Have children display each numeral on the Cuisenaire Place Value Chart with Powers of Ten materials. Ask which is greater and which is less. Review the symbols >and< and have a child insert the correct symbol. Repeat for other similar pairs of numerals. Write 0.5 and 0.48 on the chalkboard. Have children display each numeral on Master 2 with Powers of Ten materials and tell which is greater or less. Have a child insert the correct symbol on the chalkboard. Write 0.3 and 0.31 and repeat the procedure. Continue with other similar pairs of numerals.

Develop a generalization for comparing decimals: begin at the place with the highest value. If the numerals are the same, compare the digits in the next highest place. Repeat for other pairs of numerals and include pairs such as 0.26 and 0.31 where the smaller numeral requires more Powers of Ten pieces than the larger one. Continue the activity, comparing 3-digit decimals and mixed numerals. Include pairs like 0.04 and 0.004; 2.4 and 2.04; 0.10 and 0.01.

EXTENSION: On Master 2, use dimes and pennies to compare tenths and hundredths; bills, pennies and dimes to compare mixed numerals.

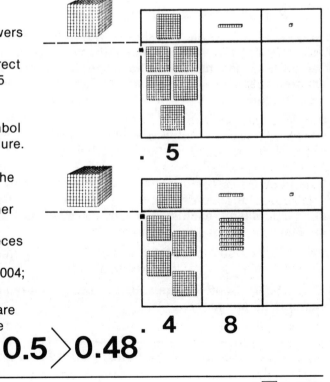

. 5

. 4   8

0.5 > 0.48

Activity 84: Rounding Decimals

MATERIALS: Money and Master 2.
Repeat Activity 14 using decimal notation for money.

Activity 85: Adding Decimals

MATERIALS: Powers of Ten Blocks, Cuisenaire Place Value Chart, Money, Masters 2 and 18.
LET ORANGE CUBE = 1 WHOLE

Write 1.3 + 3.5 on the chalkboard. Have children display each numeral with Powers of Ten materials on the Cuisenaire Place Value Chart, and then "Add" the pieces together. Record the sum. Discuss the adding procedure used with the material. Have a child write the example on the chalkboard in vertical form and solve. Repeat for several similar examples. Write 2.31 + 1.4 on the chalkboard and follow the same procedures to solve and record. Discuss the importance of lining up the digits in the vertical example. (Since like things are added together, ones, tenths, etc. must be lined up.) Repeat with several similar examples, then with three-digit decimals. Use examples that require exchanging and regrouping.

VARIATION: Use money on Master 2 instead of using Powers of Ten materials.

EXTENSION: Repeat the activity, having children use Powers of Ten materials to solve examples, but record on Master 18. Use examples with 3 or more addends to give children experience in setting up column addition for "ragged" decimals. Use Master 18 to record.

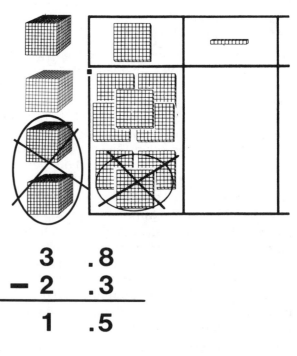

$$\begin{array}{r} 1\ .\ \ 3 \\ +\ 3\ .\ \ 5 \\ \hline 4\ .\ \ 8 \end{array}$$

Activity 86: Subtracting Decimals (Making Change)

MATERIALS: Powers of Ten Blocks, Cuisenaire Place Value Chart, Money, Masters 2 and 18.
LET ORANGE CUBE = 1 WHOLE

Write 3.8 − 2.3 on the chalkboard. Have children solve the example using Powers of Ten materials on the Cuisenaire Place Value Chart. Record on the chalkboard in vertical form. Have children solve 2.5 − 1.36 using materials. Review the trading process. (See Activity 12 and 13 for a discussion of subtraction with regrouping.) Write the example in vertical form on the chalkboard. The algorithm should be an exact parallel of the procedures used with materials. Repeat for several other examples.

Using Powers of Ten materials, have children solve other "ragged" subtraction examples which use one to three-place decimals. Record each example, being sure that the algorithm parallels the actions on the materials.

VARIATION: Use money (bills and coins) and Master 2. Examples like $8.00 − $3.56 are models for "making change".

EXTENSION: Continue the activity, having children record each example on Master 18.

$$\begin{array}{r} 3\ .8 \\ -\ 2\ .3 \\ \hline 1\ .5 \end{array}$$

Activity 87: Estimating Decimal Sums and Differences

MATERIALS: Powers of Ten Blocks, Cuisenaire Place Value Chart, and Master 2.

Follow the procedures described in Activities 15 and 16, applying them to decimals.

Activity 88: Decimals and Fractions

MATERIALS: Fraction Circles Set, Masters 10-12, and 16.

Have children use fraction circles cut from Masters 10-12. Do NOT cut the tenths circle into sectors. Ask children to solve the following by placing the indicated pieces on the uncut tenths circle: 1/2 = ?/10; 2/5 = ?/10. Have them write the appropriate decimal for each answer (0.5, 0.4), and record on Master 16. Use other fractions such as 2/4, 1/5, ... 5/5; 3/6, 4/8, 2/2, finding their equivalents in tenths.

VARIATION: Reverse the procedure, having children use the fraction circles to find equivalent fractions for 5/10, etc.

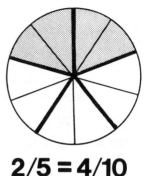

2/5 = 4/10

Activity 89: More Decimals and Fractions

MATERIALS: Fraction Circles, Orange Flats, Masters 10-12 and 14, Scissors and Crayons.
LET ORANGE FLAT = 1 WHOLE

Review the value of each square marked on the flat (1/100 or 0.01). Relate the flat to the grids on Master 14, calling each grid "one whole" and each square 1/100 (0.01). Have children cut out the four grids, fold one in half, and color one of the halves. Ask what part of the whole is colored (1/2), how many hundredths are colored (50). Have children write a fraction and a decimal on the grid to describe this relationship. On the chalkboard write 1/2 = 0.50 and discuss.

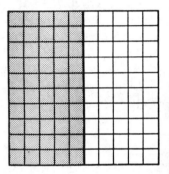

Have children fold another grid into fourths, and color one fourth. Using the fraction circles, have children place the 1/4 piece on the circle divided into tenths. Ask how many tenths the 1/4 covers ($2\frac{1}{2}$ tenths). Ask how many hundredths in 1/2 tenth (5 hundredths), in $2\frac{1}{2}$ tenths (25 hundredths). Record on chalkboard as 1/4 = 0.25. Check this solution by referring to the grid folded into fourths and counting the hundredths that were colored (25). Compare the two models used. Repeat the activity for other fractions using one or both models. Additional discussion will probably be needed for thirds and sixths.

Activity 90: Decimals and Percent

MATERIALS: Masters 14, 19, Orange Flat, Crayons.
LET ORANGE FLAT = 1 WHOLE

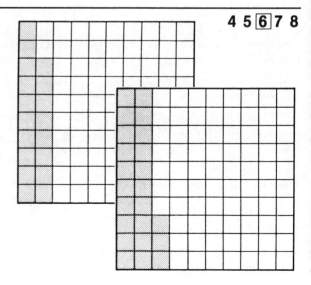

Discuss the meaning of percent (out of one hundred). Have children color 0.18 on Master 14. Ask children to tell the total number of squares on the grid (100) and how many squares were colored out of 100 (18). Explain that another way of saying "18 out of 100" is 18 percent, and that it is written as 18%. Write 0.18 = 18% on the chalkboard. Repeat with other decimals.

Write 23% on the chalkboard. Have children color in the appropriate number of squares on Master 14 and tell the decimal equivalent. Record on the chalkboard. Repeat for other percents. Discuss the similarities and differences in notation between a decimal and its corresponding percent.

EXTENSION: Call out a fraction. Have children "find" the appropriate decimal (See Activity 89 above) and then the percent.

Use Master 19. Have children find the percent each diagram is of an orange flat.

Activity 91: More Decimals and Percent

MATERIALS: Powers of Ten Blocks.
LET ORANGE CUBE = 1 WHOLE

Review the meaning of percent and the fractional part each Powers of Ten piece is of the orange cube. Write 0.13 on the chalkboard. Have children display 0.13 using the materials and then write the percent (13%). Write 0.132 on the chalkboard. Have children display 0.132 with the materials and compare the two displays (0.132 has two more unit cubes than 0.13 or 13%). Have children display 0.14 with the Powers of Ten materials and ask them to tell the percent (14%). Elicit that 0.132 is between 0.13 and 0.14, or between 13% and 14%. Discuss changing 0.132 to percent, bringing out that the two unit cubes are two tenths of the orange rod, and that 0.132 should be written as 13.2%.

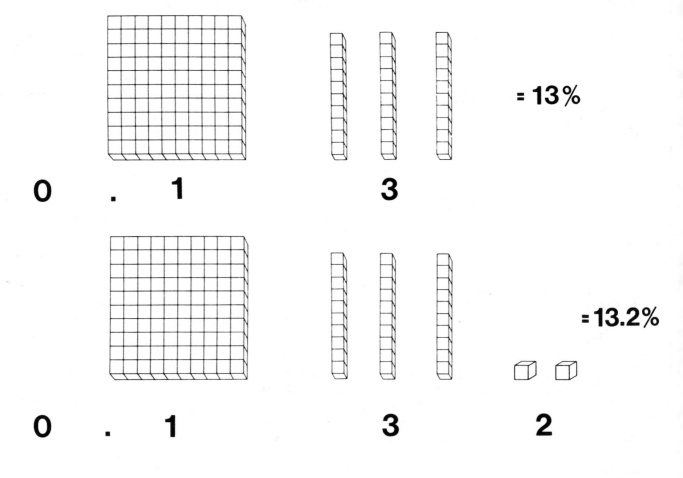

GEOMETRY

Activities 92-107

Activity 92: Points and Line Segments

4 5 6 7 8

MATERIALS: Geoboards, Rubberbands, Tape.

Have children put a strip of tape below each row of pegs on the geoboard. Beginning with A at the top left peg and moving across the row, have children letter each peg in alphabetical order. Have them point to peg H, then show it on the chalkboard as a dot labeled H, (Ḣ) and call it "Point H". Repeat with several other points. Have children use one rubberband to connect points B and X. Show this on the chalkboard as B̶̶̶̶̶X and call it a line segment. Show the symbol for the line segment as B̲X̲. Ask them to show a variety of line segments such as G̲H̲, M̲R̲, etc. Discuss the similarities among the line segments formed and have children define the term (i.e. a straight path between 2 points). Distinguish between line segment (which has a definite beginning and ending point) and line (which goes on indefinitely in both directions).

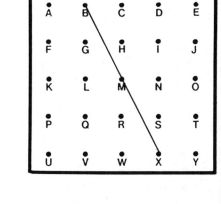

Activity 93: Parallel and Intersecting Lines

4 5 6 7 8

MATERIALS: Geoboard, Rubberbands, Master 20.

Have children form B⃗L on the geoboard, then form D⃗N. Compare the two segments, discussing their directionality and whether they might cross if extended. Extend both as far as possible and compare again. Introduce the term "parallel" to describe two lines or line segments on the same surface (place) which do not cross. Have children show G⃗M on the geoboard, find three other line segments that are parallel to it and record on Master 20. Continue similarly for F⃗B, U⃗E, etc. Have children display Q⃗T on the geoboard, then M⃗Y. Discuss the intersection of the lines, i.e. the lines intersect at a point and four angles are formed. Introduce the term "intersecting lines" to describe two lines or segments which will cross or touch. Have children show P⃗W on the geoboard, then display three line segments that intersect P⃗W. Show G⃗Q, then show a line that is parallel, and another that intersects. Record this information on Master 20. Repeat several times. Have children share their findings with the class and use the geoboard to answer questions about their solutions.

Activity 94: Perpendicular Lines

4 5 6 7 8

MATERIALS: Geoboards, Rubberbands, Master 20.

Have children display C⃗M and F⃗H on the geoboard. Ask whether the line segments are parallel or intersecting. Have children extend F⃗H to the next point so it becomes F⃗I. Discuss the special kind of angles formed at H, the point of intersection (right angles). Point out that right angles have square corners. Children may need to place a square-cornered object (i.e. index card or tile), in the corner to "see" it clearly. Introduce the term "perpendicular" to describe intersecting lines or segments which form right angles.

Have children show $\overrightarrow{DS}$ and show three line segments perpendicular to it. Record this information on Master 20. Have different children share their findings with the class. Continue similarly for $\overrightarrow{UE}$, $\overrightarrow{LD}$, etc. Introduce the symbol ($\perp$) for perpendicular and discuss its appropriateness.

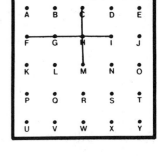

Activity 95: Identifying and Constructing Angles

4 5 6 7 8

MATERIALS: Geoboards, Rubberbands, Masters 20 and 22.

On the chalkboard, draw a right angle. Label it using letters that correspond to those on the geoboard. Have children reproduce it exactly on their geoboards. Repeat two or three times, orienting the right angle differently each time. Children should reproduce each angle in exactly the same way on their geoboards. Review the term "right angle" and discuss the square corners. Draw an acute angle on the chalkboard. Ask children if it has the same, larger, or smaller measure as a right angle. Have them make a right angle on their geoboards and use a rubberband of contrasting color to make a smaller angle with a common side, within the right angle. Compare the two angles, discussing the differences between them. Have children display several other angles smaller than right angles on the geoboard and record the angles on Master 20. Follow similar procedures to introduce angles larger than right angles.

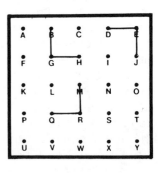

EXTENSION: Have children label the pegs on the circular geoboard from A to L, starting at the top and moving clockwise. The center peg should be labeled 0. Have them make right, acute and obtuse angles on the circular geoboard. Record each angle, using letters on a chalkboard chart. Label the chart "Right Angle", "Smaller Than Right Angles", "Larger Than Right Angles".

Introduce the term "acute angle" for those angles smaller than right angles and "obtuse angle" for those larger than right angles. Have children demonstrate a variety of each on both sides of the geoboard.

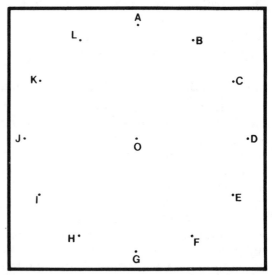

Activity 96: Identifying Complementary and Supplementary Angles

4 5 6 7 8

MATERIALS: Circular side of the Geoboard, and Rubberbands.

Have children label the circular geoboard (see Activity 95) and make angle A O G using one rubberband. Introduce the term "straight angle". Discuss the appropriateness of the name. Explain that the measure of a straight angle is 180° and have children construct other straight angles on the geoboard. Have them make angle J O D.

With a contrasting colored rubberband, make angle A O D. Ask for the special names for angles J O D and A O D (straight angle, right angle); the number of degrees in each (180°; 90°); and which two angles together form angle J O D (J O A, and A O D). Explain that when two adjacent angles form a straight angle, they are called supplementary angles. Ask for the sum

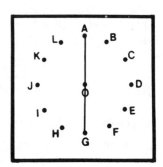

of angles J O A and A O D (180°) and elicit that these angles are supplementary. Have children construct angle H O J on the geoboard, find an angle supplementary to it (angle H O D or J O B), and prove their findings (i.e. show that the two angles are adjacent and that together they form a straight line). Repeat for angles L O B, K O C, and F O E.

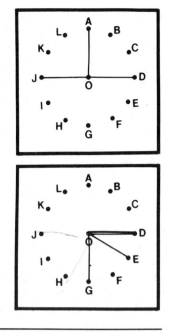

Have children make angle D O E and then with a contrasting colored rubberband, make angle D O G. Ask for the special name for angle D O G (right angle) and its measure (90°); the special name for angle D O E (acute angle); and name of the adjacent acute angle (E O G). Explain that when two adjacent angles form a right angle (i.e. have a sum of 90°), they are called complementary angles. Have children make angle K O A on the geobaord, find its complement (K O J or A O B) and prove the answer. Repeat for angles C O D, H D F, and L O K.

EXTENSION: Have children find a complementary and a supplementary angle to a given angle, e.g., angles I O H, E O G, etc.

Activity 97: Developing the Concepts of Simple Closed Curves and Polygons on the Geoboard

4̲ 5 6 7 8

MATERIALS: Geoboards, Rubberbands, Master 20.

Have students use one rubberband to make a Z (connect points B, D, L and N on the geoboard). Ask them to trace the curve with their finger. Discuss where the curve begins and ends, and introduce the term "open curve". Have them form several other open curves. Record one of them on Master 20 and label it "open curve". Draw ⌐⌐, Ꝭ , △ on the chalkboard and have children use one rubberband to make each on the geoboard. Compare these figures to an open curve, emphasizing that these end and begin at the same point. Introduce the term "closed curve". Have children use one rubberband to make several other closed curves. Record one of them on Master 20 and label it "closed curve".

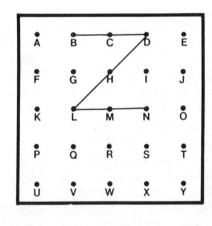

Draw a rectangle and a triangle on the chalkboard and have children make these on the geoboard. Ask if these are open or closed curves. Discuss how these closed curves differ from the Ꝭ , (do not cross themselves) and use the term "simple closed curve" to describe the rectangle and triangle. Have children show several other simple closed curves on the geoboard. Point out that the rectangle and triangle are composed of line segments only. Introduce the term "polygon" to describe a simple closed curve made of line segments. Have children form polygons with 3, 5, 4, 6, etc. line segments; with 4 line segments having two sides parallel; with 5 line segments having no sides parallel; with 3 line segments having one side perpendicular; etc. Each of these polygons should be recorded and labeled on Master 20.

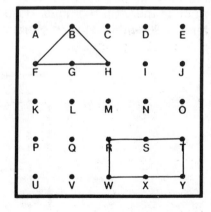

Activity 98: Developing Quadrilaterals on the Geoboard

4 5̲ 6 7 8

MATERIALS: Geoboards, Rubberbands, Master 20.

Have children use one rubberband to make a polygon with four sides on the geoboard and record it on Master 20. Compare the different figures created. Introduce the term "quadrilateral" to describe any four-sided polygon, pointing out that the prefix "quad" means four. Have children count the number of angles each quadrilateral contains. Discuss the length of the sides and the sizes of the angles, emphasizing that they may or may not be equal. Have children make a variety of four-sided figures including squares, rectangles and parallelograms and record on Master 20.

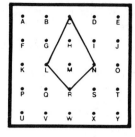

Activity 99: Classifying Quadrilaterals

MATERIALS: Geoboards, Rubberbands, Master 20.

Review the meaning of "quadrilateral" (see Activity 98), having the students make several different ones on the geoboard. Ask them to make a quadrilateral with one pair of opposite sides equal and two acute angles. Name it using the letters on the geoboard pegs. Have them record their display on Master 20. Introduce the term "trapezoid" to name this special quadrilateral and have students demonstrate several others on the geoboards. Ask them to display trapezoid B D J F on their geoboards record it on Master 20, and label the figure "trapezoid". Review which pair of sides are parallel (i.e. B D and J F).

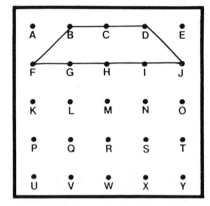

Challenge students to move the rubberband only two pegs to make the other pair of sides parallel. Have them name the new side (BDHF or BDJH), and record it on Master 20. Discuss the characteristics of the new shape (2 pairs of opposite sides are parallel), introduce the term parallelogram to describe it and have children write "parallelogram" under their recording. Have children form several other parallelograms, recording and naming each on Master 20. Discuss the size of the angles on these parallelograms.

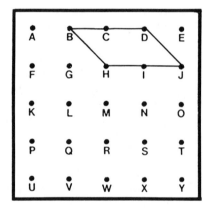

Have students display a parallelogram in which all the angles are 90° (i.e. right angles). Review the name for this figure (rectangle), and have them display several. Have them display a rectangle with four equal sides and name the figure (square). Challenge them to build a parallelogram having 4 equal sides that is not a square. Ask students to display their efforts. Introduce the term rhombus. Have them record a rhombus on Master 20 and label it "rhombus".

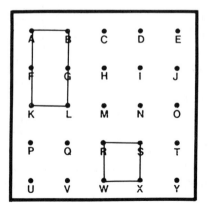

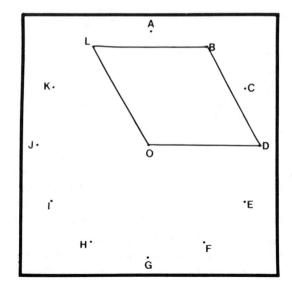

Activity 100: Classifying Triangles

MATERIALS: Geoboards, Rubberbands, Masters 20 and 24.

Have children make a triangle on the geoboard in which two sides are the same. (Measure the sides with cm rulers to be sure.) Record it on Master 20. Introduce the term "isosceles" and have children label their recording "isosceles". On their geoboards, have them make an isosceles triangle that has a right angle; an obtuse angle; 3 acute angles. Record each display on Master 20.

Have children display a triangle in which none of the sides are the same (measure the sides with the cm ruler to be sure). Record it on Master 20 and name it "scalene". Ask them to display a scalene triangle with one right angle; an obtuse angle; 3 acute angles. Record each on Master 20.

Have children display a triangle in which all of the sides are equal. (Have them measure the sides of the triangles using the cm rulers.) After experimenting, they will discover that it cannot be done on this side of the geoboard. Have them use the circular side to display this triangle and name it "equilateral". Ask them to make an equilateral triangle with one right angle; one obtuse angle. They will discover that equilateral triangles always have three equal angles and these angles can only be acute.

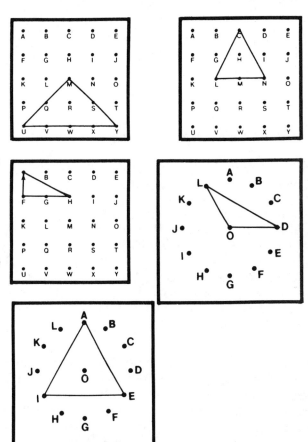

Activity 101: Radius and Diameter of A Circle

MATERIALS: Circle side of the Geoboard, Rubberbands, Masters 22 and 24.

Using the circle side of the geoboard, have students outline the circle with one rubberband and mark a letter next to each peg, as shown on Master 22. Ask them to connect the center point (0) to any point on the outside of the circle using a different color rubberband. Repeat several times and compare the length of each line segment (they are equal). Measure their lengths to the nearest centimeter to verify using the centimeter rulers on Master 24. Introduce the term "radius" to describe a line segment which connects the center of the circle to a point on the edge. Have children name each radius (e.g. OA, OH). Ask children to form as many radii as possible for this circle, count them (12), and discuss the possibilities of forming others. Record the radii on Master 22.

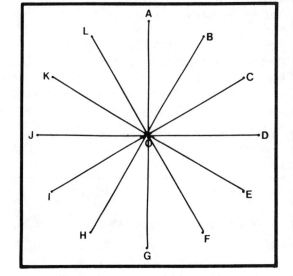

Have children display one radius on the geoboard, and extend the rubberband from the center point to the point directly opposite. i.e. OA to AG. Introduce the term "diameter" to describe the line segment that goes through the center of the circle and connects 2 points on the circle. Elicit the observations that the diameter divides the circle into 2 equal parts, and that a diameter is formed by two radii. Have children display several other diameters on their geoboards, compare the lengths (i.e. they are equal), and measure with the centimeter ruler to verify. Have children record several diameters on Master 22.

EXTENSION: Have children connect points L and D, H and C, on the circle. Ask if these line segments are radii or diameters and why (No, they do not pass through the center of the circle). The term "chord" may be introduced to describe the line segment which connects any 2 points on the circle. A diameter is a special kind of chord.

Activity 102: Circumference

MATERIALS: Geoboard, Tape Measures, Unit Cubes, Rubberbands, String, Scissors, and Master 23.

Have students outline the distance around the geoboard circle with string and cut off that length. Introduce the term "Circumference" to describe this distance. Have children place the string across the circle, from J to D, to form a diameter. Mark the end point of the diameter on the string with a pen. Have children fold the string at that point to form another diameter length and mark it; repeat as often as possible. Record the number of diameters formed on the chalkboard as "3 +" times.

On Master 23, have students place as many unit cubes as they can around the circumference of Circle A, remove the cubes and count them. Next have students draw a diameter across Circle A, and place unit cubes along the diameter, remove the cubes and count them. Record on the chart on Master 23. Repeat the procedure for Circles B and C. Have students study the entries on the chart. Discuss the relationship between the number of cubes needed for the circumference (C) and the number of cubes needed for the diameter (D) of each circle (C is always a little more than 3 times D). Introduce the expression "Pi" and the symbol π to describe this constant ratio, indicating that π = 3.14. Introduce the formula C = π D. Have children measure the diameter of each circle, and multiply by 3.14 to find its circumference (a calculator could be used).

EXTENSION: Have children measure the diameter of various coins and determine their circumference.

Review the relationship between radius and diameter (D = 2r). Have students form radius OC on the geoboard and measure its length. Have them find the circumference of the circle, substituting 2r for D. Compare with the circumference found earlier to verify that C = π D and C = 2πr are equivalent.

Activity 103: Slides and Flips

MATERIALS: Geoboards, Masters 6 and 26, Scissors, Crayons.

Have children place a coin, head side up, in the upper left hand square of the geoboard and slide it across to the upper right hand square. Introduce the word "slide" for the action and elicit from the children that in a slide the coin changes its position on the geoboard, but otherwise remains the same. Have children place another coin (tail side up) in the upper left hand square of the geoboard and slide it down to the lower left hand square. Elicit from the children that this action is also a slide.

Place a coin, head side up in the upper left hand square of the geoboard, and demonstrate flipping it over into the next square. Introduce the word "flip" for the action and elicit from the children that in a flip the coin not only changes its position on the geoboard, but also changes from a "head" to a "tail" Have children place a coin tail side up in a square on the geoboard and flip it over. Discuss the sliding and flipping activities: did the size and shape of the coins change; what changed; how are slides and flips different? Continue the activity having children work in pairs, with one child performing a slide or flip and the other identifying the action.

EXTENSION: Have children color and cut out each region on Master 26. Ask them to place Region A in the upper left hand corner of Master 6 and trace it. Have them draw a thick red line on the graph paper that is parallel to the right side of the figure. Ask children to predict where the figure will fall, and how it will look, if it is flipped "over the line". Have them flip the figure, trace it and discuss their findings. Continue similarly using the other regions from Master 26. Point out that for Regions C, D, E, and F, the flipped figure looks "different" from the original figure. Vary the position of the "red line" (i.e. parallel to the top, bottom or left side of the figure) and repeat the activity.

Activity 104: Turns

4 5 6 7 8

MATERIALS: Geoboards, Rubberbands, Master 20.

Have children work in pairs. Have each child use one rubberband to make figure G H R T Y V on his/her geoboard. Have Child One turn his/her geoboard so that the right edge of the geoboard (E...Y) moves to the bottom. Have children compare the "turned" figure and the "original" figure for size, shape and position. In the discussion, emphasize that turning a figure preserves its size and shape. However, the position or orientation of the figure changes. Have children alternate making figures and turning the geoboard.

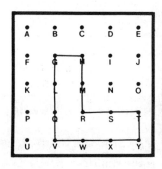

Have Child One make a figure (or design) on the geoboard, record it on Master 20, and label it "original". On the other geoboard, have Child Two make the figure as it would look after turning. Then turn Child One's geoboard to check that the two figures match. Have Child Two record his/her figure on Master 20 and label it "turned". Have children alternate roles several times.

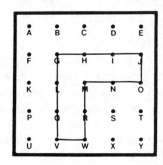

EXTENSION: Have Child One draw a figure on Master 20. Have Child Two make the "turned" figure on the geoboard. Have Child One turn the drawing and compare it with the figure on the geoboard to check. Repeat several times.

Activity 105: Developing the Concept of Symmetry

4 5 6 7 8

MATERIALS: Geoboard, Rubberbands, Masters 20, 21, Scissors.

Have children place a rubberband down the center of their geoboard (on line CW). Have them use a contrasting colored rubberband to make rectangle F J T P. Elicit that CW cuts the figure in half. To prove, have them cut out a rectangle that matches F J T P from Master 21, label it "rectangle", fold it in half, and match the paper "half-figure" to the geoboard "half-figure" (F H R P or H J T R). Have children clear the geoboards of everything, then place a rubberband across the center on line KO. With a contrasting colored rubberband have them make rectangle B D X V. Elicit that KO cuts the rectangle in half. To prove, have them fold the paper rectangle in half and match the paper "half-figure" to the geoboard "half-figure". Introduce the term symmetry. Discuss that so far they have found a rectangle to have two lines of symmetry. Reiterate that if a figure is folded on a line of symmetry, the two parts match. Ask children to find other lines of symmetry for the rectangle (there are no more).

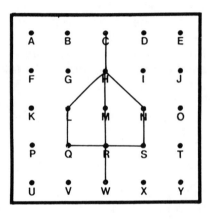

Repeat the activity using figure G I S Q. Since G I S Q is a square, it has four lines of symmetry. Discuss with children the difference between squares and rectangles.

EXTENSION: Have children work in pairs using one geoboard. Have them put a rubberband on line CW. Have Child One make half of a design on the left side of CW. Have Child Two complete the design so that it is symmetric about line CW. Have children record the completed design on Master 20. Cut out the design and fold on CW to prove that it is symmetric. Have children alternate roles. Alternate using line CW and line KO as the line of symmetry for their designs.

Activity 106: Developing the Concept of Congruence

MATERIALS: Coins, Master 29.

Have children sort a pile of coins by shape (all will be circles); by size (nickels, pennies, etc.). Discuss that sometimes objects have the same shape, but not the same size. Ask if all nickels have the same size and same shape; all pennies, etc. Prove by stacking the coins. Have children cut out the figures from Master 29 and sort by shape (triangles, squares, etc.); by size (large and small); by shape and size. The last sorting will result in pieces that are exactly alike, i.e. have the same shape and size; pieces that match each other exactly. Ask children about the measure of the corresponding angles and the corresponding sides of the pieces that match (they have the same measure). Introduce the term congruent to describe these pairs or sets of figures.

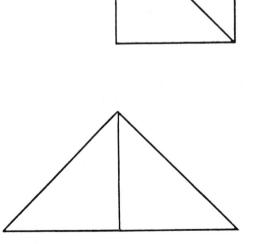

Have children fold a square in half. Ask if the 2 parts are congruent and why (yes, they have the same shape and size; the measures of the angles and of the sides are equivalent). Have children find different ways to fold a square in half to produce a congruent pair of figures. (This can be done four different ways.) Ask if all the congruent pairs obtained from folding a square are the same shape (No); what shapes are formed (rectangles or triangles). Repeat for the triangles. (The right triangle can be folded in only one way; the equilateral triangle three ways; triangular pairs always result.)

MATERIALS: Geoboards, Rubberbands, Masters 20 and 21, Scissors.

On the geoboards, have children make figure F G B with one rubberband and another figure that matches it exactly. Record the triangles that the children made on the blackboard, e.g. C G H, K L Q, N S T, etc. To prove that the two figures match, have children cut out one square unit from Master 21, cut the square along its diagonal, and "coincide" that paper triangle with each of the figures on the geoboard. Ask what motions (slides, flips, or turns) are needed to make triangle F G B "coincide" with the other triangle. Have children place the paper triangle on figure F G B and carry out the motions on the paper triangle until it coincides with the other triangle. Have several children demonstrate the motions needed to "move" triangle F G B to the other position on their geoboards. Introduce the term congruent to describe two figures that can be made to coincide exactly. Have children record both of the triangles on one "geoboard" on Master 20 and label it "congruent triangles".

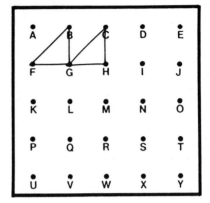

Have children make figure F I N K on the geoboard, cut out a matching rectangular strip from Master 21, make a figure congruent to F I N K on the geoboard, and prove congruence using the paper rectangle. Have several children demonstrate the motions needed to make their two rectangles coincide. Have children record both of their rectangles on one geoboard on Master 20 and label it "congruent rectangles". Reiterate the meaning of congruent figures. Repeat the procedure for other shapes: triangles (scalene, right but not isosceles, isosceles but not right), rectangles, squares, trapezoids, etc.

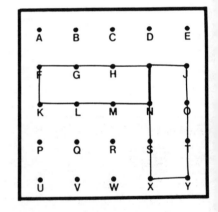

Have children work in pairs with one geoboard and alternate roles. Have Child One make a figure on the geoboard and specify 2-4 motions to be used to move it. Child Two cuts out a paper figure from Master 21 congruent to the figure on the geoboard, carries out the motions and then makes the "moved" congruent figure on the geoboard. Have children record both figures on Master 20.

MEASUREMENT (METRIC LINEAR, AREA, VOLUME)

Activities 108-120

Activity 108: Measuring with Meters and Centimeters

4 5 6 7 8

MATERIALS: Tape Measures, Masters 24 and 25, Scissors, Tape.

Have children cut the four centimeter strips A-D, from Master 24 and tape them together end-to-end to form a meter strip. Number the strip from 1-100, making sure the numbers are directly below the centimeter marks, not in the intervals. Ask how many centimeters in all. Elicit that a meter has 100 centimeters, a centimeter is 1/100 or 0.01 of a meter. Display the tape measures and have children compare them to the meter strips. Working in pairs or small groups, ask children to look around the classroom and find five items that they estimate to be about 1 meter long, five items that are about 10 centimeters long, and two items that are about 1 centimeter long. Their estimates shoudl be recorded on Master 25. Have children measure the objects to the nearest centimeter, using the meter strips or the tape measures, and then record the actual measurements on Master 25. Discuss results, comparing estimates with actual measures. If children have not listed the unit cube as an item measuring 1 centimeter, you may wish to introduce it and discuss its dimensions (1 cm x 1 cm x 1 cm). Continue measurement with meters and centimeters by having children measure the lengths and widths of the classroom, the hallway, the closets, bulletin boards, etc., always estimating first, and recording on Master 25. (These worksheets should be saved for use in Activity 110.) Have children estimate to the nearest centimeter and then measure around their own neck, waist, wrist, thumb and height. Record on Master 25.

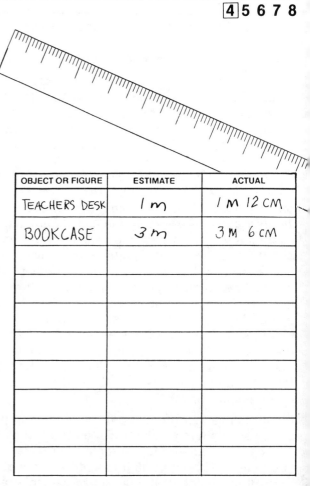

OBJECT OR FIGURE	ESTIMATE	ACTUAL
TEACHERS DESK	1 m	1 M 12 CM
BOOKCASE	3 m	3 M 6 CM

Activity 109: Measuring With Millimeters

4 5 6 7 8

MATERIALS: Masters 24 and 25, Scissors and Tape.

Have children cut out centimeter strip E on Master 24. Review the relationship between centimeter and meter using the metric strip (See Activity 108). Emphasize the decimal nature of the metric system. Compare centimeter strip E to the four others and discuss how it differs in appearance. Elicit from the children that each centimeter on strip E has been divided into 10 parts. Introduce the term "millimeter" and the symbol (mm). Have children count the number of millimeters in 2 centimeters, 5 centimeters, and 10 centimeters. Record on a chalkboard chart. Have children observe the chart and find a pattern. Develop a generalization about the number of millimeters in a given number of centimeters and a rule for changing from centimeter to millimeter. Using the rule, have children determine the number of millimeters in 15 centimeters, 25 centimeters and 100 centimeters (1 meter). Record

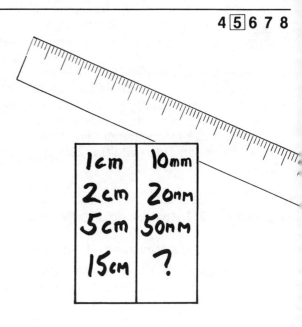

1cm	10mm
2cm	20mm
5cm	50mm
15cm	?

---

on the chalkboard. Elicit from children that there are 1000 millimeters in 1 meter; 1 millimeter is 1/1000, or 0.001 of a meter. Have children try to find five objects in the room that measure about 1 millimeter; 5 millimeters and record on Master 25. (Some possibilities are the edge of a cardboard game box; a dime; a line drawn by sharp pencil point.) Have them measure the objects with the millimeter ruler and record the actual measure. Discuss results, comparing estimates with actual measurements.

Activity 110: Place Value, Adding and Subtracting

4 5 6̲ 7 8

MATERIALS: Tiles, Tape Measures, Masters 2, 18 and 25.

The children will need to refer to the data they recorded on Master 25 during Activities 108 and 109. (If these activities were not done, have children measure objects in meters and centimeters for use in this activity.) Label Master 2: 10 Meters; Meters; Tenths of a Meter; Hundredths of a Meter. Have children make the line between the "Meter" and "the Tenth of a Meter" column heavier. Use red tiles for 10 Meters, green tiles for Meters, blue tiles for Tenths and yellow tiles for Hundredths. Write the measurements recorded for the length or width of the classroom on the chalkboard, i.e. "12 meters 45 centimeters". Ask where the separation between the whole unit and the fractional part should be and have a child draw a line between the 12 meters and the 45 centimeters. Have children decide how to display the 12 meters (i.e. how many 10 meters, how many meters). Place one red tile and 2 green tiles in the appropriate columns. Discuss how to display the 45 centimeters, (relate to previous experiences with tenths and hundredths and dimes and pennies). Place 4 blue tiles in the Tenths column and 5 yellow tiles in the Hundredths column. Read the display as "12 and 45 hundredths meters" and record it numerically as 12.45m.

Relate the verbalization and decimal recording to the original data; have children show 0.45m on the meter strip (See Activity 108) or tape measure to reinforce their understanding that 45 centimeters is read as 45 hundredths of a meter. Repeat the procedure with several other measurements recorded on Master 25. Have one child indicate his/her height measurement (e.g. 143 cm) and discuss which columns on the chart would be needed and why. Have all the children display it with the tiles and record as a decimal. Have a second child give a height measurement and ask all to display it. Combine the two "heights" to find the sum. Record each height on the chalkboard in decimal form and carry out the addition. Continue similarly having the children use the tiles to find sums and differences for measurements they have collected, recording each action as an addition or subtraction example on Master 18.

10 METERS	METERS	1/10 METER	1/100 METER

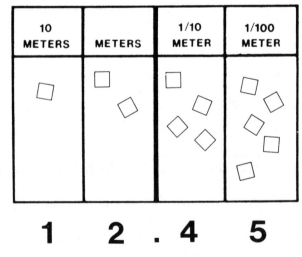

10 METERS	METERS	1/10 METER	1/100 METER

1 2 . 4 5

Activity 111: Introduction to Perimeter

4̲ 5 6 7 8

MATERIALS: Tape Measures, Master 25, String and Scissors.

Review the meaning of perimeter as the "distance around" a figure. Discuss practical needs for finding perimeter (e.g. frame around a picture, fence around a yard, border around a curtain, etc.). Have children use string to measure the perimeter of the covers of various text books, cutting the sting for each measurement. Have them stretch out the string, estimate its length in centimeters, and then measure it against the tape measure or meter strip (See Activity 108) to find its actual length. Record the estimated and actual measurements on Master 25. Have children estimate and measure other book covers, or different objects, with perimeters greater (or less) than those recorded.

Activity 112: Perimeter Using the Geoboard

4 5 6 7 8

MATERIALS: Geoboards, Rubberbands, Master 20.

Have children work in pairs or groups of 3, sharing one geoboard. If the geoboard has not been used before, demonstrate its use. Allow children time for experimental free play. Ask children to connect 2 adjacent pegs in the same row or column with a rubber band. Define this distance as one unit. Have them show 2 units, 4 units, etc. Emphasize that the rubberbands must always be parallel to one edge of the geoboard. Have the children make a square that measures 2 units on each side and find the perimeter. (8 units). Continue, having them make squares and rectangles, with sides of specific length, finding the perimeter of each figure. Specify a perimeter and have the children create a figure of their own on the geoboard with that perimeter. Encourage them to be creative. These figures should be recorded on Master 20, with the perimeter indicated. Elicit from the children that the perimeter of a figure is the sum of the lengths of its sides.

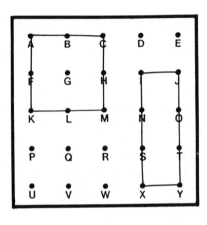

Activity 113: Measuring Perimeter in Centimeters

4 5 6 7 8

MATERIALS: Tape Measures, Masters 6, 24, 25 and 26.

Have children estimate the perimeter of each figure on Master 26 and record it on Master 25. Order the figures by perimeter, estimating length from longest to shortest, and record on the chalkboard. Have them measure the perimeter of each region to the nearest centimeter with a ruler cut from Master 24, and record the actual measurements. Discuss the difficulty of estimating the perimeter of irregular figures.

EXTENSION: On Master 6, have children draw as many figures as they can with a perimeter of 12 cm, 18 cm, 26 cm, etc. These figures may be colored if desired and each should be labeled with its perimeter. Encourage children to be creative. However, they must be able to calculate the perimeter accurately and explain, if requested.

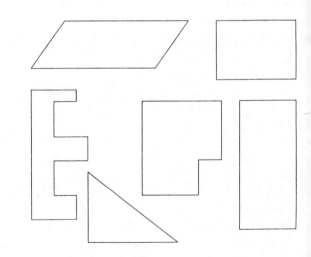

Activity 114: Introduction to Area

4 5 6 7 8

MATERIALS: Coins, Tiles, Master 26.

The children should work in 4 groups, with each group being given a different coin to use (i.e. pennies, nickels, dimes, quarters). Have them look at Figure A on Master 26 and estimate the number of coins needed to cover it. Cover the figure with coins, and count. The estimated and actual number

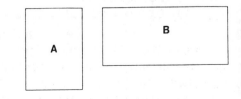

of coins should be recorded on a chalkboard chart by group. Discuss the different results of each group, which coins were better to use, and why. Continue, having each group use tiles instead of coins on Figure A. Again, record estimated and actual measurements on the chart. Repeat the activity, using Figures B and C. Discuss the results. Compare the tiles and coins to decide which is a better unit for covering and why. (Tiles, because they are squares.) Explain that they have been finding the area of regions. Ask them to try to define area in their own words. Try to elicit the idea that area is concerned with covering a surface.

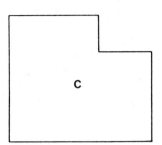

Activity 115: Area on the Geoboard

$\boxed{4}$ 5 6 7 8

MATERIALS: Geoboards, Rubberbands, Masters 20 and 21, Scissors.

Have children cut out squares from Master 21. Define each as one square unit. Have them use the paper squares on the geoboard to show figures with an area of 2 square units, 3, 4, etc.; outline each figure with a rubberband and remove the paper squares. Discuss how the square units within each figure can be counted. Display one square unit on the geoboard using one rubberband. Have children form rectangular figures of 4, 5, 6 square units, etc. Have them create other figures on the geoboard, cover with paper squares, count the square units, and record each figure on Master 20.

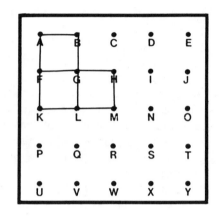

Activity 116: Discovering the Formula for Area

$\boxed{4}$ 5 6 7 8

MATERIALS: Scissors, Masters 6, 24 and 26.

Have children describe each unit (box) on Master 6 by shape (square), and size, (1 cm x 1 cm). Define each box as one square centimeter. Introduce the symbol cm^2. Ask children to ESTIMATE the number of cm^2 in figures A, B, C on Master 26, then cover each figure with squares cut from Master 6. Cover the figures on Master 26 with squares cut from Master 6, and record the results on a chalkboard chart. Have children use the cm ruler from Master 24 to measure the length and width of figures A and B and enter the data in the appropriate columns on the chart. Ask them to look for a pattern across each row of the chart. Generalize the formula for the area of a rectangular figure as L x W. Have them apply the formula by measuring the length and width of various objects such as one flat from the Powers of Ten materials, one piece of paper currency, a spinner, etc. Compute the areas.

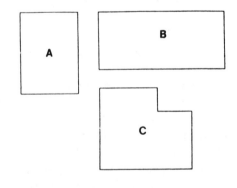

Activity 117: Finding the Area of Right Triangles

4 $\boxed{5}$ 6 7 8

MATERIALS: Geoboards, Rubberbands, Master 21, Scissors.

From Master 21, have children cut out 1 square unit and label it A; cut out 2 and 3 square unit rectangles and label them B and C, respectively. Have children draw a diagonal on each rectangle, cut along each diagonal and label the resulting pair of triangles with the same letter as the original rectangle. Elicit that two right triangles were cut from each rectangle. Discuss the relationship between the area of the original rectangle and its pair of right triangles, eliciting that each right triangle has 1/2 the area of its original rectangle.

Have children make a rectangle L N S Q with one rubberband on the geoboard. With a rubberband of a contrasting color, have them make a diagonal and cover one of the resulting triangles with paper triangle B. Elicit from children that the area of triangle B is 1/2 the area of the rectangle, or one square unit. Record on a chalkboard chart labeled "Area of Rectangle" - "Area of Right Triangle".

Have children use 1 rubberband to form a rectangle containing 12 square units on the geoboard (i.e. B E O L or C E T R, etc.) and cut a matching "paper rectangle" from Master 21. Use a rubberband of a contrasting color as a diagonal. Elicit that two right triangles with equivalent area are formed. Compare the area of each to the area of the original rectangle (one-half). Calculate the area of each triangle (1/2 of 12 or 6 square units). Have children prove that the area of the right triangle is equal to 1/2 the area of the rectangle by cutting the "paper rectangle" along its diagonal and showing that the two resulting triangles are equivalent.

Repeat this procedure for rectangles with areas of 8, 4, and 16 square units. Record the area of each rectangle and its corresponding right triangle on the chalkboard chart. Have children observe the pattern and develop the generalization that the area of a right triangle is equal to 1/2 the area of its corresponding rectangle.

EXTENSION: Relate the length and width of the rectangle to the base and height of the corresponding right triangle. Develop the formula for the area of a right triangle as 1/2 (base x height) or 1/2 b h.

Activity 118: Finding the Area of Parallelograms

4 5 6 7 8

MATERIALS: Geoboards, Rubberbands, Master 21, and Scissors.

Review that the area of a right triangle is equal to 1/2 the area of its corresponding rectangle (see Activity 117). From Master 21, have children cut out 10 separate square units, cut two of them in half along their diagonal and label each of the 4 right triangles formed "1/2 square unit". Have them cut out 2, 3, and 4 unit "strips" from Master 21; cut each in half along its diagonal and label the resulting pair of right triangles with its appropriate area. (i.e. 1 square unit, 1 $\frac{1}{2}$ square units, 2 square units). Have children label the pegs on the geoboard from A to Y (see Activity 92). Review the properties of parallelograms (see Activity 99) and have children construct and name various parallelograms on the geoboard using one rubberband.

Have children make figure H J N L on the geoboard, fill in the figure with the appropriate paper squares and triangles and determine its area (2 square units). With a contrasting-colored rubberband, have them make rectangle G I N L and compare the two figures. Elicit that both have the same area (2 units) and ask children to prove their findings (the pieces forming H J N L can be rearranged to form G I N L). For both figures discuss the base (the same, LN) and the height (the same, 1 unit). Repeat the activity for parallelogram B D R P and rec-

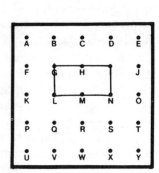

tangle A C R P, F I T Q and G J T Q: B E X W and B E T V.
Elicit that the formula for finding the area of a rectangle
(A = b x h) can also be used to find the area of a
parallelogram.

EXTENSION: Have children make figure F E T U. Ask them to
name the figure (parallelogram) and prove their answer. Ask for
the base (F E or U T), height (F U or E T), and area (12 square
units) and have children prove it using paper pieces. Repeat for
other parallelograms with bases that are not parallel to the bottom of the geoboard.

Activity 119: Introduction to Volume

MATERIALS: Masters 27 and 28, Scissors, Tape, Unit Cubes.

Have children cut out the nets for boxes on Masters 27 and 28
and tape them together. Display one of each of the boxes constructed, in a random order. Have children order them from
smallest to largest. Discuss the criteria the children used to
decide and record the final decision on a chalkboard chart.
Have children, working in small groups, estimate and then fill
each box with unit cubes. Record the estimates and actuals on
the chart. Discuss which box held the most, the least. Save the
information for Activity 120. Introduce the term "Volume" to
describe how much a container will hold when it is filled. Have
the children use the cubes to build figures with a volume of 12
cubic units in as many ways as possible. Repeat for 6, 8, 16,
etc. cubic units.

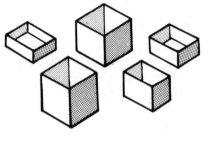

Activity 120: Developing the Formula for Volume

MATERIALS: Powers of Ten Blocks, Worksheets 24, 27 and 28,
Scissors, Tape, Unit Cubes.

Use the boxes constructed for Activity 119. (If the boxes were
not constructed, have the children do so from the nets on
Masters 27 and 28.) Discuss the shape of the cubes used to fill
the boxes and identify their dimensions (i.e. length, width and
height). Introduce the term "cubic centimeter" to describe one
of the cubes and the symbol cm^3. Relate the exponent "3" to
the 3 dimensions of the cube (length, width and height) just as
the "2" in cm^2 referred to the 2 dimensions of the square units
(length and width). If Activity 119 was done, use the volumes
discovered for each box. If not, have students estimate, then
fill each box with cm^3 to find the volume. Record the volume of
each box on the chalkboard chart. Have children use a cm ruler
(Worksheet 24) to measure the 3 dimensions of each box (i.e. L,
W, H). Record the measurements on the chart in the appropriate columns. (Reiterate that the L, W and H are all in centimeters.) Ask to look across each row of the chart for a pattern. Have them generalize a definition for volume as L x W x H
= V. Have children estimate the volume of the orange cube in
the Powers of Ten set, then measure its dimensions and find
its volume (i.e. 1,000 cm^3). Ask them to "prove" their answer
using the Powers of Ten materials.

BOX	L	W	H	Volume
A	6	4	1	24 cm^3
B				
C				
D				
E				
F				

PROBABILITY

Activities 121-125

Activity 121: Probability: Flipping Coins

4 5 6 7 8

MATERIALS: Pennies, Master 30.

Discuss heads and tails on the penny. Demonstrate flipping a coin. Have children label the first two-column tally chart on Master 30, "H" and "T". Flip a penny, and record the outcome as a tally mark in the appropriate column on the tally chart. Children take turns flipping and recording for 10 rounds, then count the number of heads and tails recorded. Add the total number of heads and tails for the whole class and discuss the results. Emphasize that the probability of getting either a head or tail is equaly likely, i.e. 1 out of 2.

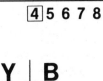

Activity 122: Probability: Using a Spinner

4 5 6 7 8

MATERIALS: Four and Five-Sector Spinners, Master 30.

Have children label a four-column tally chart on Master 30 "R", "G", "Y", "B". Children spin the spinner and record the outcome by placing a tally mark in the appropriate column. Continue the activity for 60 rounds. Total the outcomes and discuss the implications as in Activity 121. The probability of the spinner pointing to any of the four colors is equally likely, i.e. 1 out of 4. Compare these results to the results obtained from flipping a coin.

R	G	Y	B
IIII	III	Պ+I+I	IIII

VARIATION: Repeat the activity using the five-sector spinner labeled 1, 2, 3, 4, 5 and the five-column tally chart similarly labeled. (The probability of the spinner pointing to any of the five numbers is equaly likely, i.e. 1 out of 5.)

Activity 123: Probability: Using a Nonequal Spinner

4 5 6 7 8

MATERIALS: Five-sector spinner, Master 30.

On the white rim surrounding the five-sector spinner, label two adjacent sectors blue. Mark the three remaining sectors red, green and yellow. Discuss the "new" spinner with the children, asking how many colors appear. Have them theorize about the possible outcomes of using this spinner. Have children label the four-column tally charts on Master 30, B, R, G, Y and spin the spinner. Record the outcome by placing a tally mark in the appropriate column. Continue the activity for 40 rounds, total the outcomes and discuss. The probability of the spinner pointing to blue is 2 out of 5, while for red or yellow it is 1 out of 5. (There is twice the chance for the spinner to point to blue as to either of the other colors.) Discuss whether the probability of getting blue would change if the two blue sectors were not adjacent. Relabel the spinner and repeat the activity. Discuss why there is no difference.

On the white rim surrounding the five-sector spinner, designate two sectors red and three sectors green. Have children predict outcomes, then use the spinner for 40 rounds, recording on the two-column tally chart on Master 30.

Draw spinners divided in various ways on the chalkboard (e.g. four sectors, with two sectors of one color, one each of two other colors). Have children predict outcomes, explaining their reasoning.

Activity 124: Probability: Picking Tiles

MATERIALS: Red and Blue Tiles, Master 30.

On Master 30, have children label a two-column tally chart "R" and "B". Playing in pairs, children use one red and one blue tile. The "Picker" closes his/her eyes; the "Mixer" mixes the two tiles; the "Picker" takes one tile. The outcome is recorded by placing a tally mark in the appropriate column on the tally chart. Continue the activity for 12 rounds, with children rotating roles. Total the number of tally marks for red and blue tiles for the whole class and discuss the implications (as in Activity 121). Repeat the activity for 20 rounds using four tiles of different colors. Have children record on the four-column tally chart on Master 30. Have them predict the outcomes for situations using five or six different color tiles.

EXTENSION: Repeat the activity using from three to ten tiles, varying the number of tiles of each color (e.g., 5 red, 3 blue or 2 red, 2 yellow, 3 blue, 3 green, etc.). Have children label the appropriate tally chart and predict the possible outcomes before starting. Continue the activity for 30 rounds. After the activity, discuss results and implications.

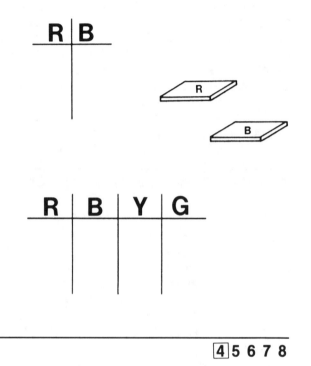

Activity 125: Probability: Picking Letters or Numerals

MATERIALS: Tiles, Crayons, Master 30.

Use a crayon or marker to label four tiles, each with a different letter of the alphabet. Repeat Activity 124. Continue similarly, labeling five tiles, two with numerals and three with letters. Have children label a five-column tally chart appropriately. Repeat Activity 124, first discussing possible outcomes of: picking a specific letter and/or numeral; any letter; any numeral. Have children do the activity and discuss results and implications.

Write each letter in the word M I S S I S S I P P I on a separate tile. Have children predict the number of different outcomes possible and the probability of each occurring before repeating Activity 124. Have children record a four-column tally chart on Master 30. There are 4 possible outcomes: the probability (P) of picking (M) is one in 11 (1/11); P (I) is 4/11; P (S) is 4/11; P (P) is 2/11. Repeat with other words or use numerals which have repeated digits, for example 35, 315.

PLACE VALUE RECORDING SHEET

THOUSANDS	HUNDREDS	TENS	ONES

THOUSANDS	HUNDREDS	TENS	ONES

THOUSANDS	HUNDREDS	TENS	ONES

THOUSANDS	HUNDREDS	TENS	ONES

THOUSANDS	HUNDREDS	TENS	ONES

THOUSANDS	HUNDREDS	TENS	ONES

THOUSANDS	HUNDREDS	TENS	ONES

THOUSANDS	HUNDREDS	TENS	ONES

THOUSANDS	HUNDREDS	TENS	ONES

THOUSANDS	HUNDREDS	TENS	ONES

FOUR COLUMN PLACE VALUE CHART

NUMBER LINE

0 1 2 3 4 5 6 7 8 9 10 11 12 13 14 15 16 17 18 19 20 21 22 23 24 25

0 1 2 3 4 5 6 7 8 9 10 11 12 13 14 15 16 17 18 19 20 21 22 23 24 25

0 1 2 3 4 5 6 7 8 9 10 11 12 13 14 15 16 17 18 19 20 21 22 23 24 25

0 1 2 3 4 5 6 7 8 9 10 11 12 13 14 15 16 17 18 19 20 21 22 23 24 25

0 1 2 3 4 5 6 7 8 9 10 11 12 13 14 15 16 17 18 19 20 21 22 23 24 25

X	0	1	2	3	4	5	6	7	8	9	10
0	0	0	0	0	0	0	0	0	0	0	0
1	0	1	2	3	4	5	6	7	8	9	10
2	0	2	4	6	8	10	12	14	16	18	20
3	0	3	6	9	12	15	18	21	24	27	30
4	0	4	8	12	16	20	24	28	32	36	40
5	0	5	10	15	20	25	30	35	40	45	50
6	0	6	12	18	24	30	36	42	48	54	60
7	0	7	14	21	28	35	42	49	56	63	70
8	0	8	16	24	32	40	48	56	64	72	80
9	0	9	18	27	36	45	54	63	72	81	90
10	0	10	20	30	40	50	60	70	80	90	100

INSTRUCTIONS:

1. Make two copies of this Master and cut out the "halves" of the cube.

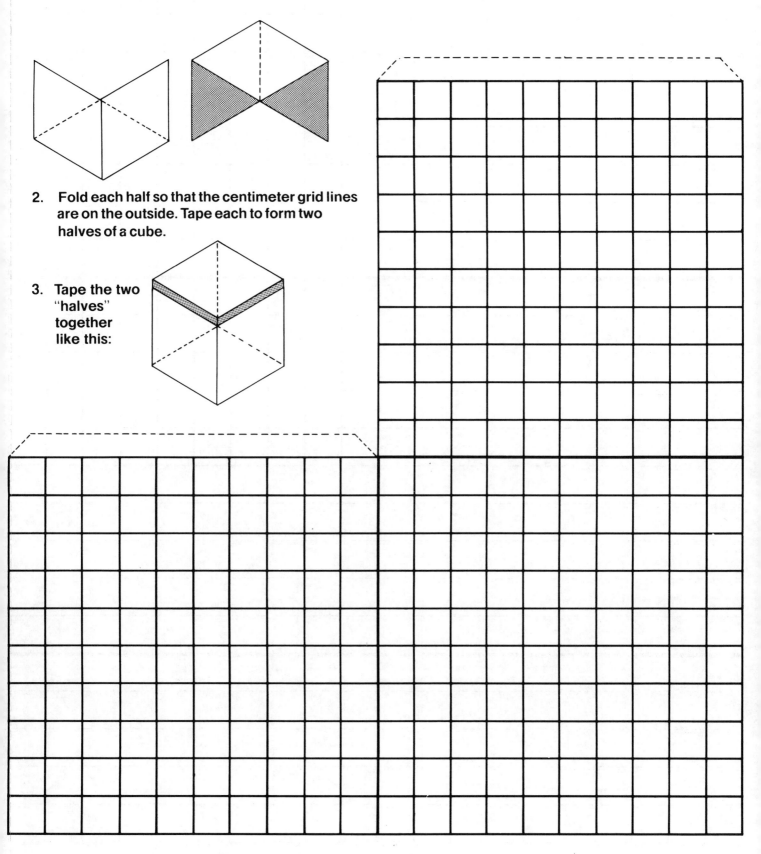

2. Fold each half so that the centimeter grid lines are on the outside. Tape each to form two halves of a cube.

3. Tape the two "halves" together like this:

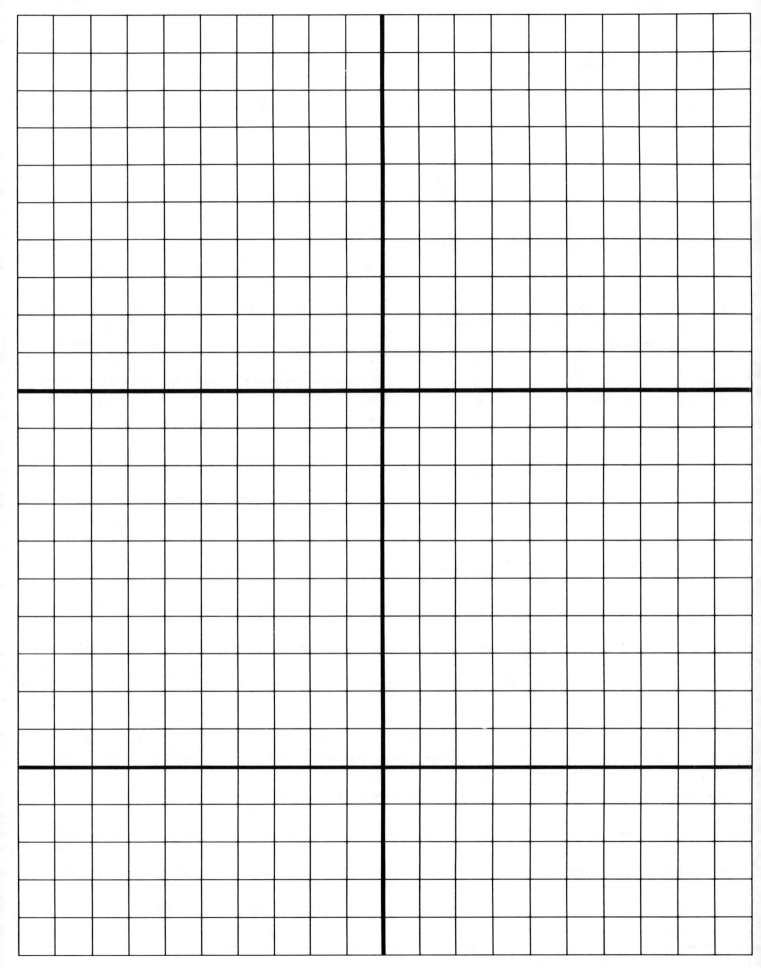

91	92	93	94	95	96	97	98	99	100
81	82	83	84	85	86	87	88	89	90
71	72	73	74	75	76	77	78	79	80
61	62	63	64	65	66	67	68	69	70
51	52	53	54	55	56	57	58	59	60
41	42	43	44	45	46	47	48	49	50
31	32	33	34	35	36	37	38	39	40
21	22	23	24	25	26	27	28	29	30
11	12	13	14	15	16	17	18	19	20
1	2	3	4	5	6	7	8	9	10

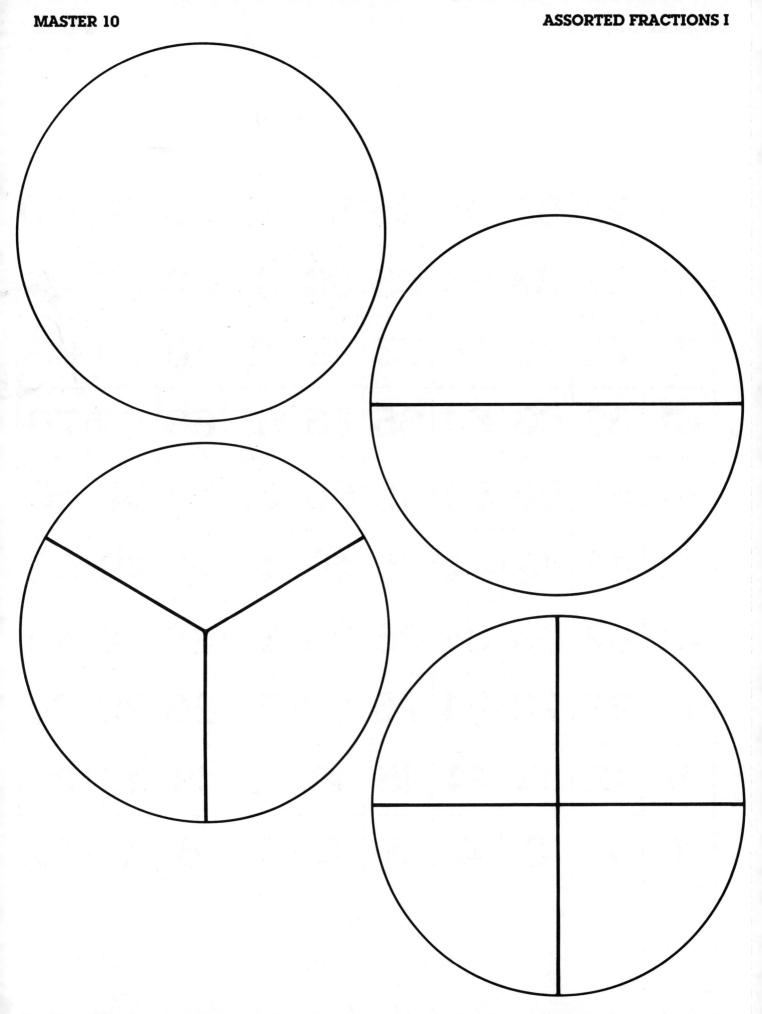

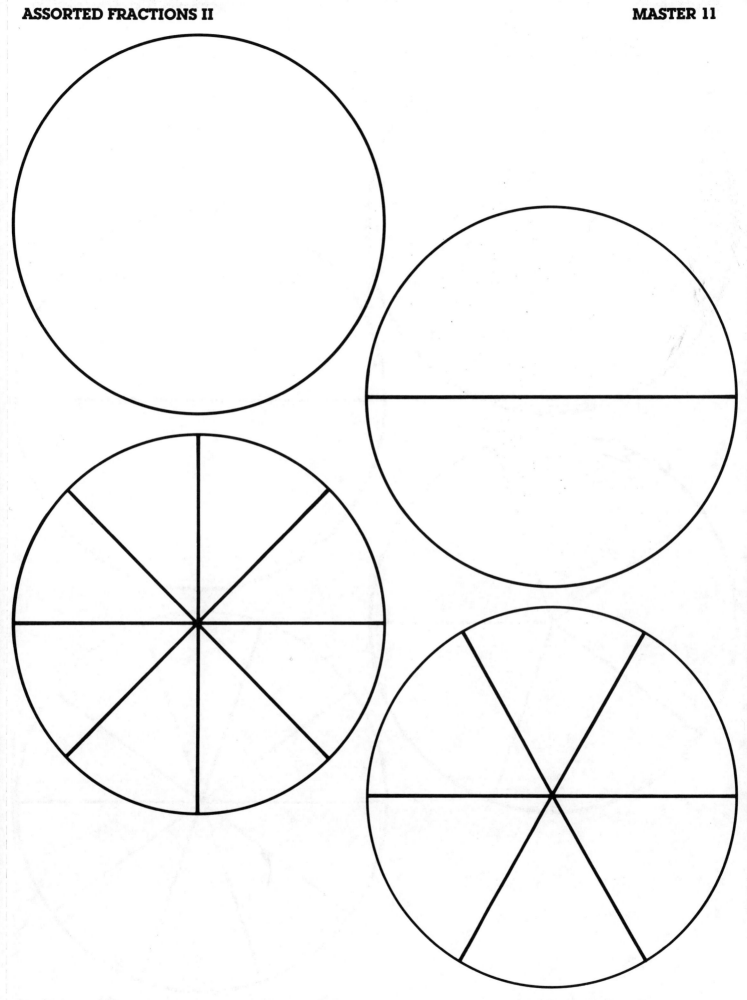

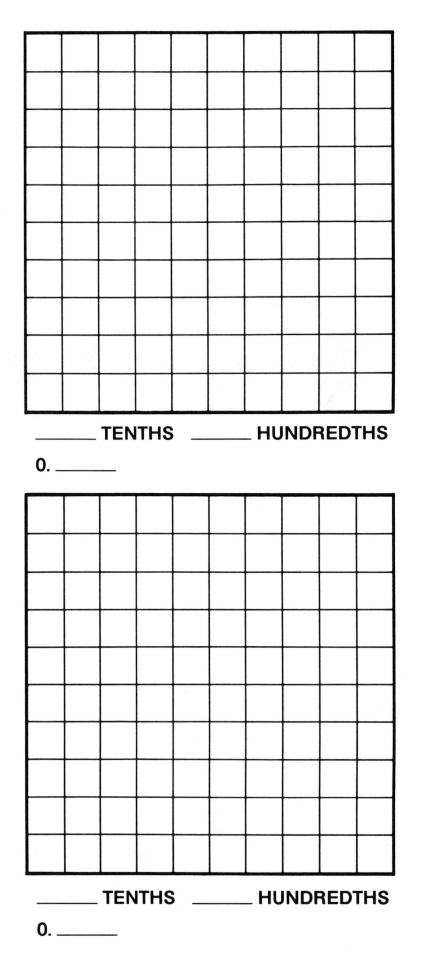

_____ TENTHS _____ HUNDREDTHS

0. _____

_____ TENTHS _____ HUNDREDTHS

0. _____

LET THE ORANGE FLAT = 1 WHOLE

Cover each shape with flats, orange rods and/or white cubes. Write the fraction and the decimal for each.

Fraction: _____

Decimal: _____

Fraction: _____

Decimal: _____

Fraction: _____

Decimal: _____

Fraction: _____

Decimal: _____

Fraction: _____

Decimal: _____

Fraction: _____

Decimal: _____

Hundreds	Tens	Ones	Tenths	Hundredths	Thousandths
		.			

Hundreds	Tens	Ones	Tenths	Hundredths	Thousandths
		.			

Hundreds	Tens	Ones	Tenths	Hundredths	Thousandths
		.			

Hundreds	Tens	Ones	Tenths	Hundredths	Thousandths
		.			

Hundreds	Tens	Ones	Tenths	Hundredths	Thousandths
		.			

Hundreds	Tens	Ones	Tenths	Hundredths	Thousandths
		.			

Hundreds	Tens	Ones	Tenths	Hundredths	Thousandths
		.			

Hundreds	Tens	Ones	Tenths	Hundredths	Thousandths
		.			

Hundreds	Tens	Ones	Tenths	Hundredths	Thousandths
		.			

Hundreds	Tens	Ones	Tenths	Hundredths	Thousandths
		.			

Hundreds	Tens	Ones	Tenths	Hundredths	Thousandths
		.			

Hundreds	Tens	Ones	Tenths	Hundredths	Thousandths
		.			

LET THE ORANGE CUBE = 1 WHOLE

Cover each shape with flats, orange rods and/or
white cubes. Write the fractions and the decimal
for each.

Fraction: _____

Decimal: _____

Fraction: _____

Decimal: _____

Fraction: _____

Decimal: _____

Fraction: _____

Decimal: _____

Hundreds	Tens	Ones	Tenths	Hundredths	Thousandths

Hundreds	Tens	Ones	Tenths	Hundredths	Thousandths

Hundreds	Tens	Ones	Tenths	Hundredths	Thousandths

Hundreds	Tens	Ones	Tenths	Hundredths	Thousandths

Hundreds	Tens	Ones	Tenths	Hundredths	Thousandths

Hundreds	Tens	Ones	Tenths	Hundredths	Thousandths

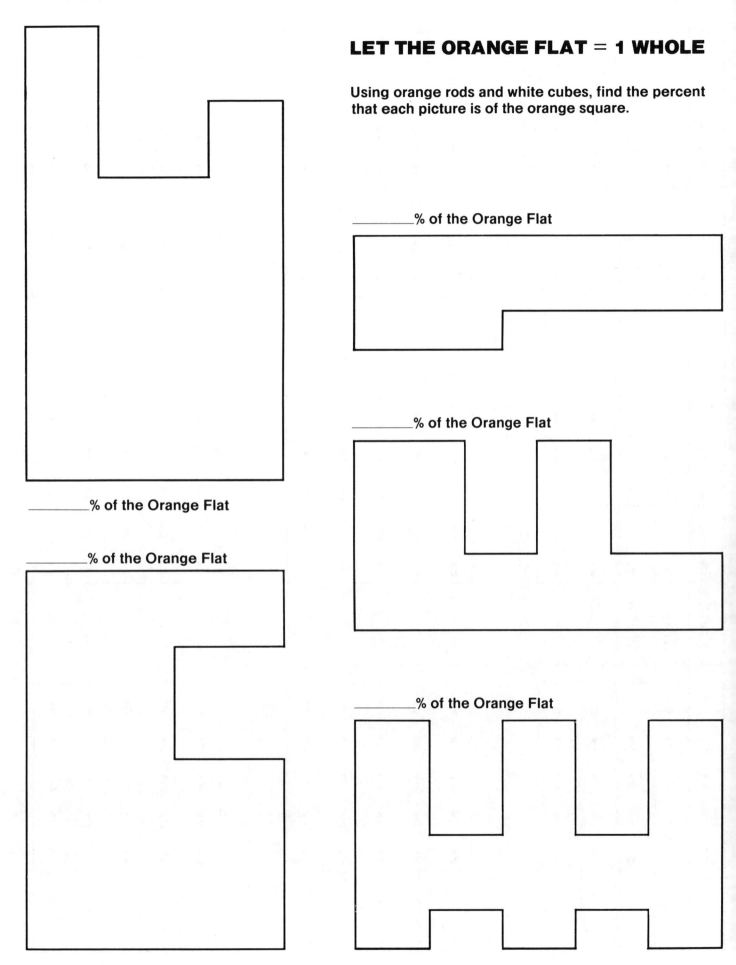

LET THE ORANGE FLAT = 1 WHOLE

Using orange rods and white cubes, find the percent that each picture is of the orange square.

_____% of the Orange Flat

_____% of the Orange Flat

_____% of the Orange Flat

_____% of the Orange Flat

_____% of the Orange Flat

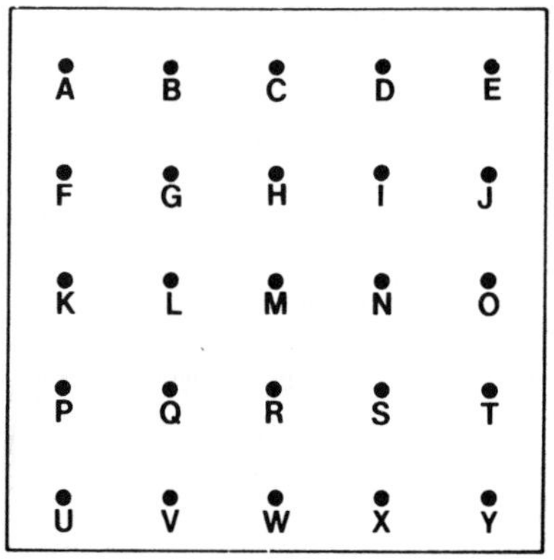
A B C D E
F G H I J
K L M N O
P Q R S T
U V W X Y

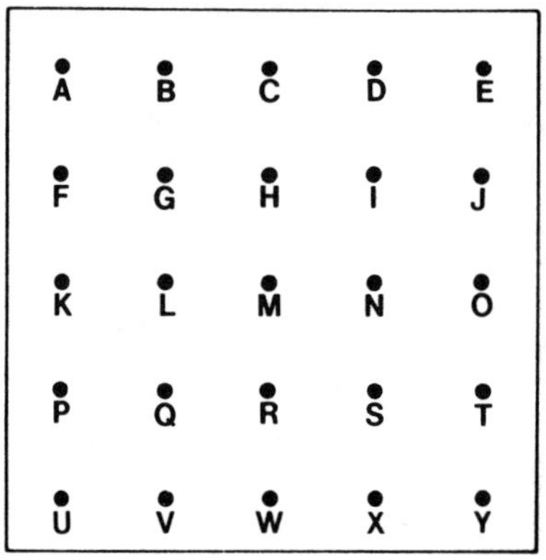
A B C D E
F G H I J
K L M N O
P Q R S T
U V W X Y

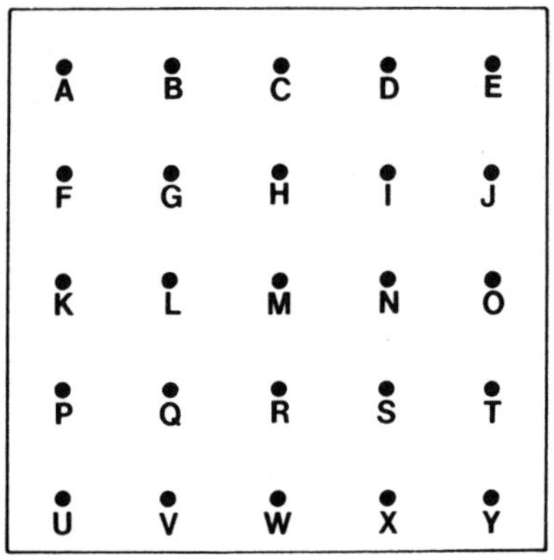
A B C D E
F G H I J
K L M N O
P Q R S T
U V W X Y

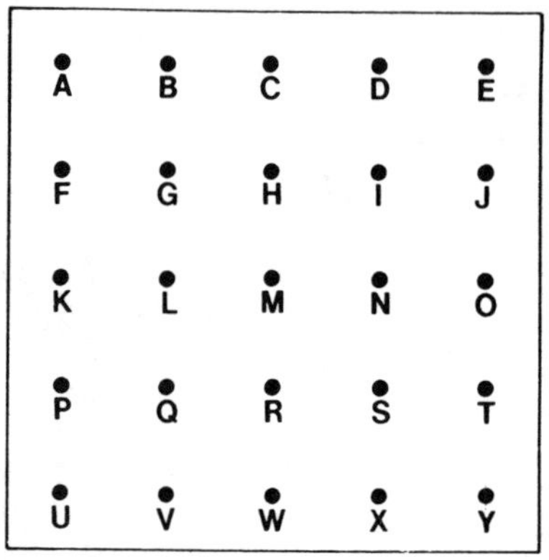
A B C D E
F G H I J
K L M N O
P Q R S T
U V W X Y

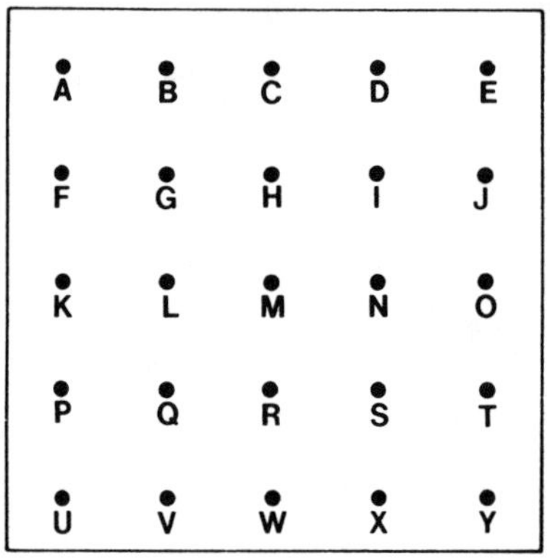
A B C D E
F G H I J
K L M N O
P Q R S T
U V W X Y

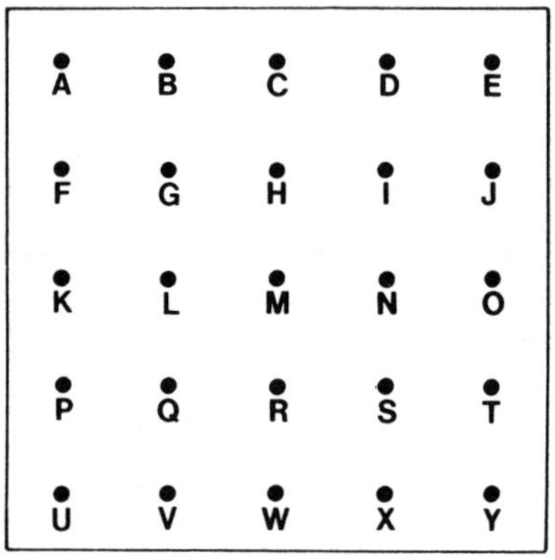
A B C D E
F G H I J
K L M N O
P Q R S T
U V W X Y

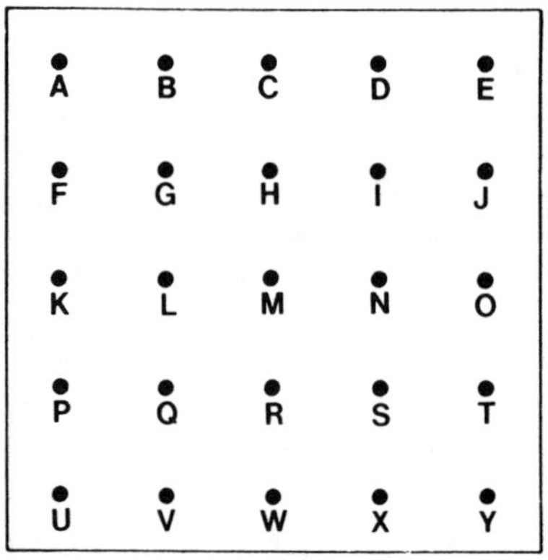
A B C D E
F G H I J
K L M N O
P Q R S T
U V W X Y

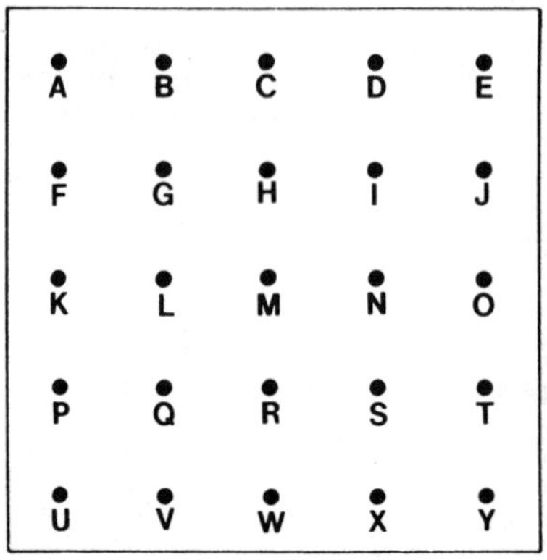
A B C D E
F G H I J
K L M N O
P Q R S T
U V W X Y

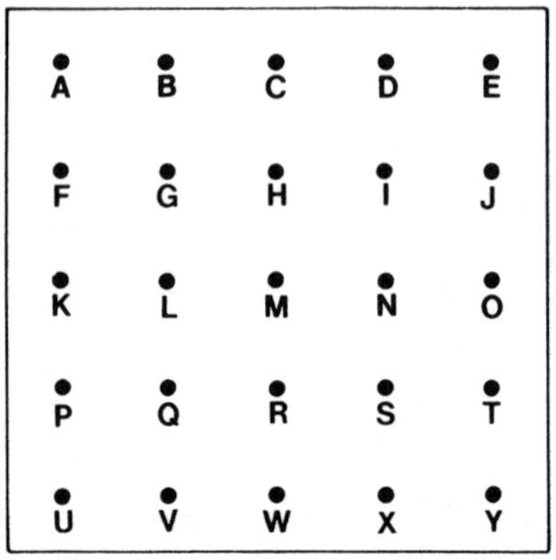
A B C D E
F G H I J
K L M N O
P Q R S T
U V W X Y

A
●

L
●   B
                                                         ●

K●   ●C

J●   ●   ●D
                                O

                                                              ●E

                        ●   ●
                        H   F

                                ●
                                G

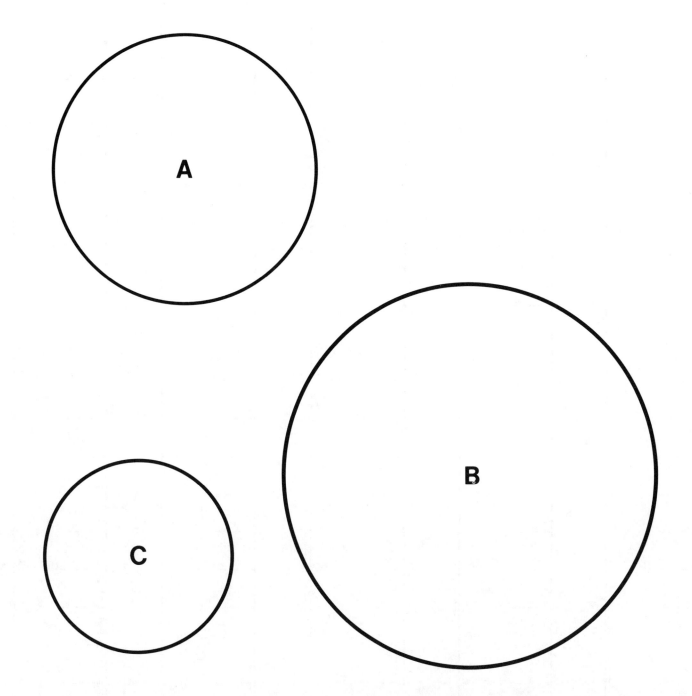

NUMBER OF UNIT CUBES			
Circle	Circumference	Diameter	$\frac{C}{D}$
A			
B			
C			

A   B   C   D   E

NAME:

OBJECT OR FIGURE	ESTIMATE	ACTUAL

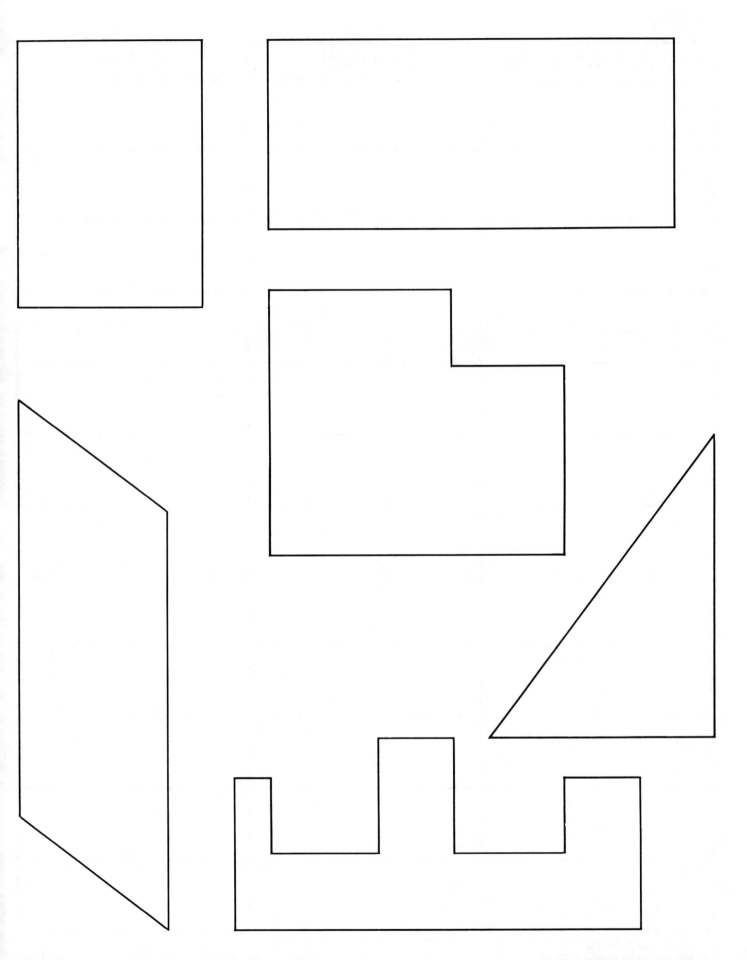

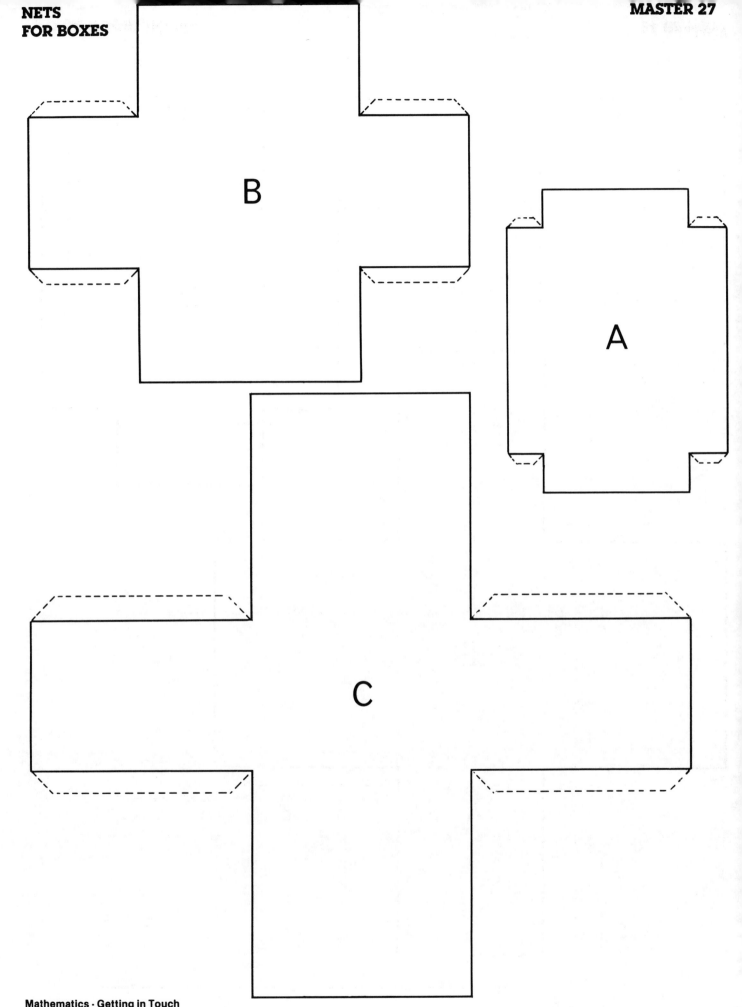

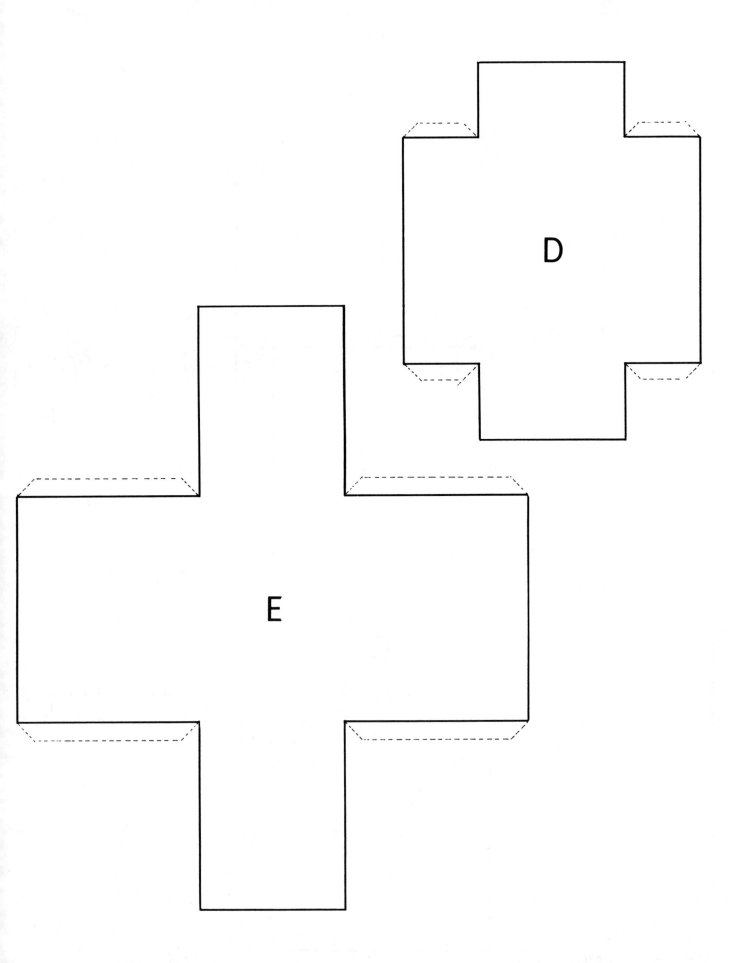

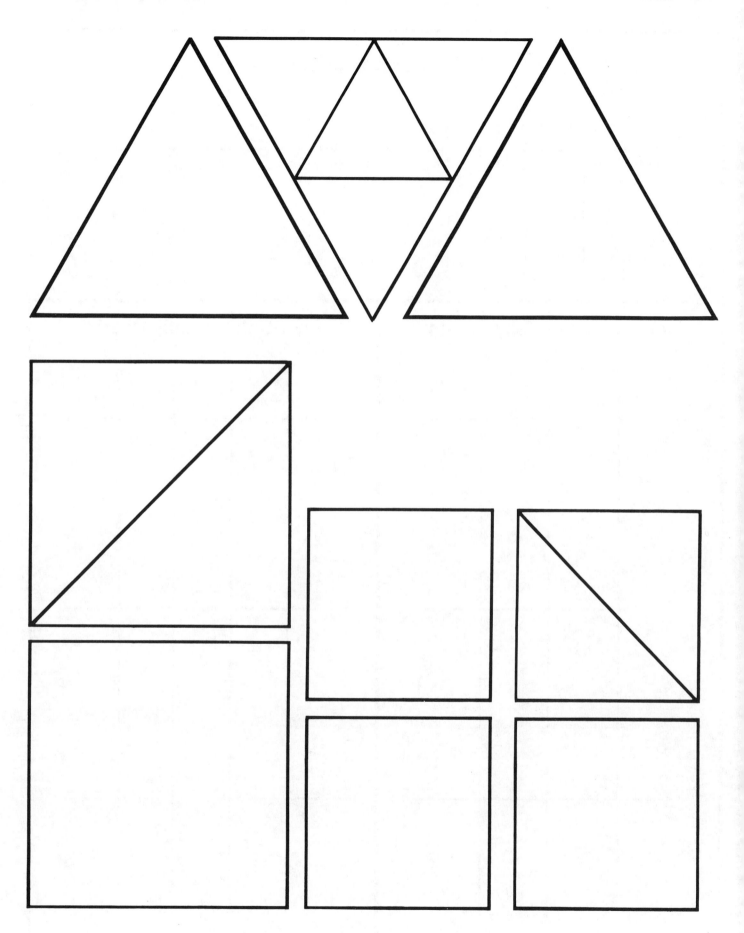

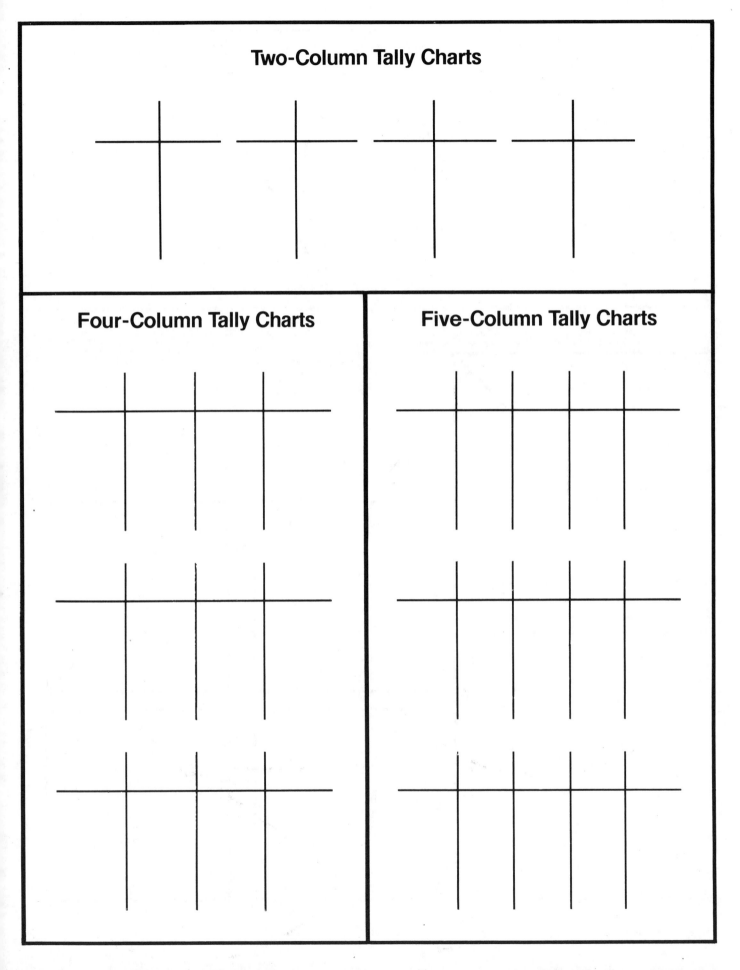

Two-Column Tally Charts

Four-Column Tally Charts

Five-Column Tally Charts